PRODUCTIZE IT!

FROM IDEATION
TO IMPLEMENTATION

I0440224

MANAL HADDAD

TO MY MOTHER

DISCLAIMER

Copyright © 2021 Manal Haddad.

All Rights Reserved. No part of this book may be reproduced, stored, or transmitted by any means – whether auditory, graphic, print, photocopying, scanning, mechanical, or electronic – without written permission of the author, except in the case of brief excerpts used in critical articles and reviews. Unauthorized reproduction of any part of this work is illegal and punishable by law.

ISBN: 978-1-4466-8442-9

Because of the dynamic nature of the Internet, any web addresses or links contained in this book may have changed since publication and may no longer be valid. The views expressed in this work are solely those of the author and do not necessarily reflect the views of the publisher, and the publisher hereby disclaims any responsibility for them.

All the information mentioned herein is based on thorough research and the author's experiences. Any mention of specific institutions, public offices, and long-standing agencies is made by name because of their role in the relevant industry and the services they offer.

Any opinions expressed here are not meant to be critical, harmful, or derogatory in any manner. The greatest efforts have been taken to ensure the accuracy of all factual details in the written content.

All information, ideas, and guidelines presented here are for educational purposes only. Readers are encouraged to seek professional advice when needed.

While the author has made the utmost effort to ensure the written content's accuracy, the author cannot be held responsible for any personal or commercial damage caused by misinterpretation of the information contained herein.

The advice mentioned in this book is not a substitute for any professional advice from established professional leaders and consultants in the field.

The book is intended for informational purposes only and should be treated as such. You should not make any financial decisions based solely on the content of this book without consulting an expert.

CONTENTS

ABOUT THE BOOK

Every year, thousands of new products are launched into the market, and while some fail to make it big, others become game-changers and disrupt the status quo. With the right approach and knowledge, any product can be successful, and it takes courage and determination to bring a new idea to life. As an entrepreneur, you have the power to educate yourself on the successful development, launch, and roll-out of your product to ensure its success.

Productize It! From Ideation to Implementation is the ultimate guide for product developers and entrepreneurs. This comprehensive book provides a step-by-step manual to navigate the complex concept development, commercialization, and launch process. It enables them to avoid critical mistakes and create an attractive brand that stakeholders across the value chain will want to purchase and use.

With this book, you will have everything you need to transform your FMCG product idea into a global success and avoid common pitfalls most product developers make while getting faster traction. By equipping yourself with the knowledge outlined in this book, you can bring your FMCG product to market and achieve the success you deserve.

If you aspire to create a successful product, get it on store shelves, and win over the hearts of consumers, you have come to the right place. This book will guide you through the entire process and help you bring your innovative ideas to life. If you diligently follow the guidelines and suggestions in this book, rest assured that your product will come to life and attain remarkable success!

CHAPTER 1

WHAT IS A PRODUCT?

Let us start our discussion on creating and selling products by clarifying what a product is. A product is a tangible or intangible item made directly from labor, effort, or a process. The term "product" comes from the verb "produce," derived from the Latin prōdūce (re), which means "(to) lead or bring forth." It has been in use since 1575 and has evolved to encompass anything that can be produced.

In this book, "product" refers to an item produced, packaged, and labeled for sale. This standardized and manufacturable object can be placed on a shelf in a brick-and-mortar store or made available for purchase online. Our usage of the term is unambiguous, leaving no room for confusion or misinterpretation.

A product is more than just an item or service you sell to fulfill a customer's need or want. As you will discover in this book, it has multiple attributes and benefits beyond what meets the eye and what the customer initially expects to pay for. In essence, a product is a powerful tool that can cater to your customers' needs in ways they may not have imagined.

Undoubtedly, the term "product" encompasses a wide range of elements. From a marketing perspective, a product is anything that can be sold to a market to satisfy a need or want. It is important to note that in the world of retail, products are known as merchandise, while in manufacturing, they are purchased as raw materials and sold as finished goods.

WHAT ARE FMCG PRODUCTS?

Fast-moving consumer goods (FMCG), also referred to as consumer packaged goods (CPG), are products that sell quickly and at a low price point. These products typically have a short shelf life due to their perishable nature (such as baked goods, meat, and dairy products) or high consumer demand (such as confectionary items and soft drinks). FMCG products are an essential and lucrative retail industry segment, and their popularity shows no signs of slowing down.

FMCG products are the epitome of perfect consumer goods. They are purchased frequently, consumed quickly, sold in large quantities, and come at an affordable price point. Furthermore, their high turnover rate on retail shelves is a testament to their immense popularity among consumers.

UNDERSTANDING FMCG PRODUCTS

Consumer goods refer to products purchased for personal use by regular consumers. These goods can be categorized into three main types - durable goods, non-durable goods, and services. With a clear understanding of the different categories, it is easy to identify and purchase the consumer goods that meet your needs and preferences.

Durable products are those that can be used for more than three years, while non-durable products are those that cannot last more than a year. Fast-moving consumer goods are the largest and most significant segment of consumer goods. They have a short shelf life and are typically consumed immediately after purchase.

Fast-moving consumer goods are an essential part of our daily lives, used by individuals across the globe daily. They are inexpensive purchases that we make at supermarkets, grocery stores, warehouse outlets, and produce stands. Some examples of these goods include detergent, milk, chips, beer, soda, over-the-counter medicines such as aspirin, and toilet paper.

It is a fact that FMCG products constitute more than 50% of all consumer spending. However, it is also true that these products are low-involvement purchases. If you take a moment to think about it, consumers are more likely to proudly flaunt their smartly designed laptops or brand-new cars than a new sports drink they picked up at the grocery store.

TYPES OF FAST-MOVING CONSUMER GOODS

As discussed earlier, fast-moving consumer goods are non-durable products with a short shelf-life and are consumed rapidly. They can be categorized into various types, including:

- **Processed foods:** boxed pasta, cereals, and cheese products
- **Prepared meals:** ready-to-eat foods and meals
- **Beverages:** sodas, beers, energy drinks, juices, and bottled water
- **Baked goods:** bagels, croissants, and cookies
- **Dry, fresh, and frozen food items:** vegetables, fruits, nuts, and raisins
- **Over-the-counter drugs:** pain relievers, aspirin, and other medications that can be bought without a prescription
- **Cleaning items:** oven cleaner, glass, and window cleaner, and baking soda

- **Toiletries and cosmetics:** toothpaste, soap, shampoos, and make-up products
- **Office supplies:** pencils, pens, and markers

CREATING AND SELLING PRODUCTS

When creating and selling products, it is crucial to recognize that many players are involved, each with pre-defined roles. While you may be able to develop a formula or prototype on your own, bringing on board a reliable supplier who can help with packaging and distribution is essential. And when it comes to scaling up, you will need to tap into a network of experienced distributors, retailers, and brokers who can help you take your product to the next level. With the right team in place, there is no limit to what you can achieve in product development and sales.

With this book in hand, you will possess the kind of knowledge that most product creators and entrepreneurs lack. Armed with this knowledge, you will be well-prepared to navigate the intricacies of the market and succeed in even the most competitive industries. Although new products often fail, mainly from inexperienced or new companies, you can be assured that you have the tools and insights to beat the odds and thrive.

Achieving success with your product can bring about tremendous benefits. Not only will it generate a highly profitable and long-lasting revenue stream, but in case of a sale, you can expect a remarkably favorable valuation, typically ranging from four to six times the revenue. This implies that reaching a revenue target of $2 million could potentially land you a sale worth $8 to $12 million.

CHAPTER 2

IDEATION AND RESEARCH FOR NEW PRODUCTS

BRINGING TOGETHER THE ENTIRE TEAM TO LEVERAGE THE IDEAS, EXPERIENC-ES, AND INSIGHTS OF PRODUCT DESIGNERS, DEVELOPERS,OWNERS, ARCHI-TECTS, AND QA.

The ideation phase is often called the fuzzy front-end of innovation, but it is also the most crucial stage in the product development process. It is a powerful tool that must be used at the initial stage of the product development process. Ideation generates ideas about a product in an open and creative environment. It can help discover new product concepts and methods of solving market problems or development challenges.

The goal of ideation is to allow free thinking to prevail and consider ideas that might come across as absurd or unusual yet could potentially result in exciting breakthroughs and innovations. By embracing ideation, businesses can approach product development knowing they have explored every possible avenue and considered every conceivable idea.

Your product team will significantly benefit from structured ideation sessions that facilitate collaboration and the combination of innovative thinking and creative abilities. By clearly defining the goal of the ideation session and outlining the specific challenges that need to be addressed, everyone involved will better understand how their input can contribute to the project's success. With a solid framework in place, your team can generate a wide range of ideas and solutions to drive your product's growth and success.

THE PRODUCT IDEATION PROCESS

Product ideation is crucial for any entrepreneur, product developer, or product team. To ensure its success, three essential steps must be followed: idea generation, idea selection, and actual implementation. These steps involve establishing clear criteria for judging the generated ideas, identifying the right people to review them, and finalizing the process for selecting the best ideas to be implemented or discarded. Additionally, assigning the ideas to the respective product lines and prioritizing them is crucial to ensure that the most promising ideas are implemented first. The key to executing the best ideas successfully lies in your or your firm's ability to select and follow through with them efficiently until completion.

1. IDEA GENERATION SOURCING

To generate innovative product features, you can tap into two distinct classes of idea sources - internal and external. With many options at your disposal, you can explore and experiment with different ways to inspire your creativity and come up with groundbreaking ideas.

A. INTERNAL SOURCES

To achieve successful product innovation, internal sources play a crucial role. Your Research & Development department and other internal employees from different departments are excellent internal sources. The IT/engineering department, customer service team, and sales force are some of the internal sources that regularly interact with customers and follow industry trends.

When the C-Level sets the ground for innovation, they take the first and most crucial step towards successful product innovation. The leadership's attitude towards developing a safe space for creativity significantly incentivizes employees to innovate. For instance, Toyota's leadership encourages creativity by reducing some of the pressure for short-term gains. This approach has helped Toyota invest in its brand Prius for ten years, ultimately developing a reputation for the organization as an esteemed product innovator.

B. EXTERNAL SOURCES

Your consumers and customers are your greatest assets when finding valuable information from external sources. Bill Gates says even your unhappy customers can provide you with the most significant insights. Competition is another source that you should never underestimate. However, social media is the most potent external information source, especially for product categories where customers are highly involved. It enables product developers to discover unsolicited feedback from thousands, or even millions, of customers and use it to improve their products. With the advancement of text analytics and natural language processing technologies, marketers can now effectively monitor online conversations and extract valuable insights for new product development.

P&G's "consumer pulse" is an excellent example of cutting-edge social listening. By automatically scanning online comments and using advanced methods such as Bayesian inference to classify them by brand, this tool enables P&G's marketers to promptly respond to consumers or engage in real-time online discussions. Not only does this technology help refine marketing efforts and create better products, but it also reinforces P&G's commitment to providing exceptional customer service.

2. IDEATION SELECTION METHODS

Choosing an ideation method that aligns with your goals is crucial to generate the best ideas. It is equally important to consider the teams' needs, creative productivity levels, and experience with ideation sessions. Below is a list of the most effective methods that you can use to generate outstanding ideas.

A. BRAINSTORMING

Brainstorming is undeniably the most effective method for generating fresh and innovative ideas and solving complex problems creatively. The ultimate goal is to produce as many ideas as possible within a given time frame relevant to a particular issue.

All ideas generated during the brainstorming session are recorded, and the participants are strictly prohibited from making negative comments during the process. This fosters an environment where even the most unconventional ideas can be expressed and considered.

The ideal size for a brainstorming group should be between 6 to 10 people. This number provides ample space for further discussions and integrating multiple ideas.

B. FOCUS GROUPS DISCUSSIONS

Gathering a small group of individuals with diverse personalities and conducting focus group discussions effectively provide structured information. Like interviews, Focus group discussions are qualitative research that assesses perceptions and reactions toward a product or service. This enables you to gauge the type of response you can expect from a larger audience with greater certainty.

In the initial ideation stages, focus group discussions are particularly valuable in enhancing a feature or concept and incorporating consumer feedback before investing in its production.

CASE STUDY. UNILEVER: FOCUS GROUPS THAT LOOK LIKE PLAY GROUPS

Modern focus groups have come a long way. Cutting-edge researchers continuously explore innovative techniques, such as mobile apps that track consumer purchases or creative collage-making exercises, to gain deeper insights into how consumers perceive their products.

Conventional focus group techniques, where participants discuss a brand or product while researchers observe from behind, have long been criticized for their shortcomings. Researchers' presence can negatively impact the responses; one person often dominates the entire group. Moreover, increased media saturation has led consumers to give jaded answers to research questions, making it difficult to obtain accurate insights.

However, market research company Spark, led by Malinda Sanna and Terrie Koles, has taken a bold step towards overcoming these challenges by introducing Sensory Safari. This innovative collage-building practice encourages participants to create collages to express their feelings regarding a product, advertising concept, or brand. With Sensory Safari, researchers can gather more genuine, accurate, and valuable insights and better understand their target audience.

During an event for Unilever, Ms. Koles impressively organized four tables that symbolically represented the senses: sight, smell, taste, and touch. Attendees were given iPods loaded with pop music and tasked with visually expressing their thoughts on two web-based apps for Suave, a Unilever hair care product.

While creating collages, the participating women were being carefully observed by members of Unilever's team from an adjacent room. One of the collages, featuring an inverted Barbie with her arms stretched forward, gave an impression of vulnerability and loss of control. This helped the team gain a deep understanding of consumer behavior. According to David Rubin, the marketing director for Unilever's hair care line, building collages empowered the participants to speak about their feelings, even those they were unaware of, and step out of their comfort zones. This resulted in a better understanding of the consumers and their needs.

Other brands are also adopting innovative approaches to gather consumer insights, apart from the traditional focus groups. For example, during the rebranding process of Ugly Mug Coffee, their research agency requested customers to maintain journals and create family trees depicting which family members drink coffee. They were even asked to list the worst aspects of coffee and why they consume it, among other things.

Facebook Groups have become a popular tool for online focus groups, with researchers leveraging this feature to gain vital insights. Even advertising giants such as Ogilvy & Mather use Facebook to conduct focus groups for their clients, including big-name brands like Ikea, Gap, Kimberly-Clark, and Unilever. This approach has proven effective in providing valuable feedback and driving better decision-making.

C. MIND MAPPING

This ideation selection method is compelling and offers a wide range of benefits. It can be used to structure your thoughts, organize and visualize information, manage meetings, and even plan events easily and efficiently.

Mind mapping is a simple yet highly effective technique that involves writing down a central word or phrase in the center of a blank page and then inviting participants to write down anything that comes to their mind related to the central word. Developing associations and connections between ideas creates a network of associations that can help you gain valuable insights and ideas.

What is excellent about mind mapping is that it is easy to add further ideas later on at any time, allowing you to refine your thinking and focus on the most important associations and links between ideas. With this technique, you will never end up with bits and pieces of information - instead, you will have a clear and concise picture of your ideas and how they fit together.

D. SCAMPER

Generating ideas through action verbs is a powerful tool to re-shape and improve existing processes, ideas, or concepts. SCAM-

PER, an acronym for Substitute, Combine, Adapt, Modify, Put to Another Use, Eliminate, and Reverse, provides a framework to stimulate creativity and generate innovative solutions.

- **Substitute** – Consider replacing a part of your process, idea, or concept with another to determine if it leads to any improvement, such as efficiency gains. This approach can help you gain more confidence in your decisions and take bold steps toward achieving your goals.
- **Combine** – By combining different processes, ideas, or concepts into a single streamlined output, we can achieve significantly improved results with greater efficiency and confidence.
- **Adapt** – A tried and tested approach to problem-solving involves using a successful solution from one context to address a different issue. A prime example of this is the story of Netflix. Initially launched in 1999 as a DVD rental service, Netflix quickly recognized the potential of online streaming and adapted accordingly. As a result, the company has become a significant competitor to traditional TV networks, while Blockbuster, which failed to make the necessary changes, went out of business in 2013. This demonstrates the importance of being proactive and agile in adapting to changing circumstances.
- **Modify** – To create more value, it is essential to approach the problem from a different perspective and explore the changes you can make.
- **Put to Another Use** – Consider utilizing an established solution in a novel context and observe its advantages.

- **Eliminate** – Streamline processes by identifying and eliminating inefficiencies or redundancies.
- **Reverse** – Change the structure of interchangeable components of a process or idea.

By applying each of these action verbs to a problem or challenge, you can unlock new possibilities and opportunities for improvement. With SCAMPER, you can confidently identify areas for improvement, streamline processes, and create more value. So, if you want to boost your creative thinking and develop better ideas, SCAMPER is the way to go.

E. STORYBOARDING

Walt Disney Studio's creation, the storyboard, is a powerful tool that visually represents how a product can be brought to life or how a feature can function. By combining research with creativity, this method enables individuals to showcase their ideas effectively.

The storyboard achieves this by displaying quotes from the consumer, relevant images, and other pertinent information. This approach presents a situation clearly and concisely, helping establish connections between different ideas and facilitating better understanding.

3. IDEATION IMPLEMENTATION RULES

When implementing ideation, it is crucial to keep the following rules in mind to achieve the best results:

   a. Clearly define the objective or problem: A well-defined objective produces more actionable results.

   b. Always think like your customer: Put yourself in their shoes, use the product yourself, and brainstorm ways to improve it.

   c. Get the right people onboard: Build a team of experts and amateurs who share your vision and have an eye for detail.

   d. Set boundaries: While the sky's the limit, sticking to your goals is crucial for achieving maximum results.

   e. Challenge all your assumptions: Continuously reevaluate your work to avoid taking anything for granted.

   f. Ensure effective implementation: An excellent idea is only valuable if you can successfully implement it.

IDEA SCREENING PROCESS

Once you have generated a list of new product ideas, the next step is determining which ones to pursue and which to discard. Idea screening plays a crucial role in this process, as it helps to evaluate ideas and eliminate as many as possible from consideration. The goal is to end up with fewer practical and imaginative ideas. To achieve this, it is essential to follow a defined criterion that can help you make informed decisions. By considering the following factors, you can make decisions that will lead to successful outcomes:

- **Compatibility**: how compatible Is the idea with business goals?
- **Relevance**: how relevant is the idea to existing and predicted business environment and goals?
- **Assumptions**: how valid are the premises on which the idea is based?

- **Constraints**: any internal or external constraints, such as budget, resources, and dates, that can prevent your idea from turning into a reality?
- **Feasibility**: is your idea feasible according to the resources you have available?
- **Value**: what is the expected ROI of the idea?
- **Risks**: any internal or external risks, such as competition, changes in technology, or legislation, which can prevent the success of your idea?

KEY TAKEAWAY

Remember that idea generation and screening are crucial to developing a successful product. Paying close attention to this fundamental process is vital, as it ensures continuous improvement and helps to deliver precisely what your consumers need. Neglecting this step may result in an unsuccessful product that fails to meet market demands. So, be persistent in your idea generation and screening process to ensure your product's success.

CHAPTER 3

CONCEPT DEVELOPMENT AND TESTING

VALIDATING YOUR IDEA WITH POTENTIAL USERS.

Based on research, it is determined that concept development and testing is a critical two-stage phase in the development of a new product. During this process, potential buyers are presented with an idea or description of the product, also known as concept testing, to gauge their reactions and feedback. This phase allows us to determine the product's market feasibility and potential success before moving forward with the development process.

WHAT IS A NEW PRODUCT CONCEPT?

It is essential to distinguish between product idea, product concept, and product image, but many marketers tend to use these terms interchangeably. So, let us clarify. A product idea is a potential product that can be offered to the market. The product image is how consumers perceive an existing or potential product. And the product concept is a detailed and meaningful outline of your idea. Understanding these differences allows you to develop and market your products to your target audience.

Developing a new product concept is the foundation of any successful product launch. To create a winning product concept, there are a few key factors that you should consider.

1. Develop a clear and compelling description of your product from the perspective of your target consumers.
2. Create a comprehensive list of benefits and features that your product will offer.
3. Conduct thorough market research and identify your target market to help you refine your concept and make it more appealing to potential customers.
4. Account for the resources you need to bring your product to market, including design, manufacturing, and delivery.

With a solid product concept in place, you can move forward with concept development and testing to determine the feasibility of your idea.

WHAT IS CONCEPT DEVELOPMENT?

To succeed in business, developing a concept that is unique and appealing to your target audience is crucial. Concept development involves creating a comprehensive description of an idea and presenting it from the perspective of your consumers. By incorporating functional values and usability into your product concept, you can provide your customers with maximum benefits, making it a valuable addition to the market. With a well-defined concept, you can establish a strong identity for your company and gain the confidence to succeed in your endeavors.

When developing a new product or service, focusing on the best features and benefits your solution can offer is crucial. A well-defined product concept should highlight the critical aspects of your idea in terms of:

- Usability

- Convenience
- Functionality
- Quality
- Price
- Performance
- Experience
- Values.

By working on multiple concepts and selecting the most promising ones, you can increase your chances of creating a winning product that meets the needs and expectations of your target market. So, stay focused on delivering the best possible solution.

MAKING CONCEPT DEVELOPMENT A SUCCESS

Crafting a flawless product concept is an indispensable prerequisite for introducing a highly successful and pioneering product. A poorly articulated concept can impede a revolutionary idea, stopping it from debuting on a retail outlet's shelves. In contrast, a well-crafted concept can furnish a sturdy groundwork for all that ensues, from product development to market activation.

1. USE THE APPROPRIATE CHECKLIST

In concept development, marketers often feel the need to follow a rigid checklist of elements that must be included. However, remember that the quality and clarity of the information conveyed is paramount. Do not get bogged down in including all the standardized components. Instead, focus on the content that truly resonates with consumers and showcases the power of your product. To ensure you think from the consumer's perspective, rely on Nielsen's proven **Factors of Success**[1] model. By doing so, you can approach concept development knowing that you are delivering the most effective message to your target audience.

2. CLEARLY DISCUSS THE STRUGGLES

Successful and innovative products are born out of the struggles consumers face in their everyday lives. These are the circumstances where consumers must make significant trade-offs, make do with inadequate solutions, or simply not address the struggles because they do not have a solution. A product concept that clearly describes the target struggles - who is struggling and when and how they are struggling - performs 58 percent better than concepts without these details.

Providing such details strengthens the connection between your product's key benefits and attributes and the problems consumers wish to resolve. This, in turn, leads to a higher probability of consumers purchasing our products. Moreover, products that clearly discuss these details are perceived by consumers to be:

- Be more innovative
- Be more relevant
- Be a better value
- Have an advantage over similar products.

Therefore, you must describe the consumer's struggle and explain precisely how you will address them. Your product should enable consumers to easily attain something they had previously struggled with, and you should leverage unique technological or scientific advancements. Discussing the "how" strengthens

---

1 http://innovation.nielsen.com/innovationanalytics

your competitive advantage and credibility.

3. INCREASE CONSUMERS DESIRE FOR YOUR PRODUCT

Marketers often ask, "Does my product concept truly cater to a real consumer need or desire?" Shockingly, 75 percent of tested concepts fail to meet this crucial requirement.

Even if the primary idea addresses an unfulfilled consumer desire or need, transforming this idea into a comprehensive concept can be challenging and tricky. However, with the right strategies in place, there's no reason why even a fantastic idea should fail in concept form.

a. *Price Shock* – Rest assured that your idea is well-received by potential consumers eager to reap its benefits. However, when confronted with the price tag, some may hesitate and question its value. It is essential to keep in mind that while cost is a crucial factor in the product innovation process, the benefits of your product are likely to outweigh any concerns over price. By highlighting the advantages, you can instill confidence in consumers and help them realize the true value of your offering.

b. *Substandard Expression* – Crafting a compelling description for an idea may seem simple, but it requires a strategic approach to resonate well with consumers. A subpar description of an excellent idea can leave consumers with doubts about the product's purpose or the benefits it offers. Exploring a wide range of options for copy and visuals is crucial to ensure that your idea is expressed effectively.

Technologies like Nielsen's[2] concept testing platform can help you test hundreds of alternatives quickly with remarkable results. By optimizing your concepts, you can increase the likelihood of consumer desire or need by up to 76%.

4. ENSURE THE PRODUCT CONCEPT IS ALIGNED WITH YOUR MARKETING PLAN

When it comes to product concept development, it is critical to provide consumers with the same level of information they would receive once the product hits the market. This means taking a realistic approach to design, anticipating any potential communication challenges, and considering the level of marketing support you will need to offer to drive engagement and sales. Even with a limited budget, you can still create compelling concepts by focusing on your unique selling points and incorporating distinctive features that set your product apart. Conversely, adding too much information to a concept can be counterproductive, causing confusion and diluting its overall appeal. You can create product concepts that inspire consumer confidence and drive purchase intent by striking the right balance between clarity and differentiation.

5. COLLABORATION IS KEY TO GENERATING BETTER CONCEPTS

The efficacy of the phrase "two heads are better than one" cannot be overstated, especially in concept generation. Collaborating with more people offers tangible advantages, resulting in more appealing concepts to consumers. Research shows that teams of six or more members create product concepts that are 58 percent

---

2 https://nielseniq.com/global/en/landing-page/bases-optimizer/

more liked by consumers than the brand's initial or "best guess" concept. Conversely, teams of two or fewer members, the most common team size, only result in 16 percent more liked concepts than the initial concept.

In addition to expanding the team size, involving members with diverse perspectives and professional backgrounds is crucial. Doing so leads to much better concepts. For example, teams that incorporate functions beyond the insights and marketing departments create concepts that perform significantly better than those created by insights and marketing alone.

6. ENSURE THAT YOUR PRODUCT LIVES UP TO ITS PROMISE

Once you have crafted a brilliant concept, be sure to consistently refer to it during the entire process of deploying and developing your product to ensure that it fulfills its potential. A strong concept is a great beginning, but only a powerful conclusion can make it a success. So, let your concept guide you toward the ultimate triumph.

EXAMPLE OF A WELL-DEFINED PRODUCT CONCEPT – NEW CHICKEN DIPPING SAUCES

New *Chicken Dipping Sauces* are an easy and fun way for your family to love eating a wholesome chicken meal. *Chicken Dipping Sauces* are available in two yummy flavors: *Zesty* – a combination of more spicy flavors, and *Sweet* – a light, fruity flavor.

Just make chicken as you usually would and let your family members pick their favorite *Chicken Dipping Sauce*. Irrespective of how each member eats chicken – with a fork or fingers – everyone is bound to enjoy New *Chicken Dipping Sauces*.

WHAT IS CONCEPT TESTING?

Concept testing is a crucial step in the product development process, regardless of the stage you are in. By investing resources in effective concept testing, you can evaluate your ideas with consumer segments and gain valuable insights into the likelihood of their success.

Concept testing is an essential process that enables you to evaluate your target market's reaction to your proposed offering before its official launch. It involves surveying potential consumers to get their opinions on various aspects of the concept. Using this approach, you can gather vital information on the product's features, appeal, and comparison to similar products. With this information, you can make informed decisions on how to improve the product to meet the needs of your target market. This approach also helps you to determine the optimal pricing for the product, which is a critical factor in the success of any product. So, if you want to launch a product that meets the specific needs of your target market, concept testing is an essential step you should not overlook. The following are examples of some questions you can ask potential consumers:

- How much do they like the product?
- Are they interested in purchasing the product?
- How attractive do they find the product's attributes and features?
- What features do they not like?
- How well would the product rank against similar or competing products?
- How much would they be willing to pay for it?

- Is there anything they would like to change in the product?

WHY DO YOU NEED TO CARRY OUT PROPER CONCEPT TESTING?

Comprehensive concept testing is absolutely crucial, and the following reason highlights its importance.

- **Prevents You from Taking Bad Decisions**

  Your idea may be great, but your consumers ultimately judge its success. It is unlikely to be successful if they are not on board with your product concept. Testing your product concepts beforehand will help you avoid launching ineffective and unsuccessful products.

- **Allows for Flexibility**

  Concept testing offers unmatched flexibility, making it an indispensable tool for marketers. By leveraging surveys and gathering feedback from potential consumers, marketers can obtain valuable insights about various aspects of their idea, including tone, style, price, and more. This enables them to ensure that every detail is perfect before launching the product to the target market, resulting in a confident and successful product launch.

MAKING CONCEPT TESTING SUCCESSFUL

To ensure the success of your product, conducting concept testing is crucial. This is usually achieved through customized surveys aimed at recording valuable feedback from your consumers, allowing you to gain insights into their preferences.

If you are developing your concept, your team should consider the following points to ensure successful product concept testing and an effective launch.

1. SET A GOAL

To create a meaningful and effective survey, set a clear goal. Determine what you aim to achieve through the survey and the specific information you want to gather from your respondents. This approach will enable you to develop well-crafted questions and gain valuable insights into the consumers' viewpoint, making your survey successful.

2. ENSURE CONSISTENCY IN STRUCTURE

Grouping questions linked with one another on your survey is crucial for creating a seamless and efficient flow. By doing this, respondents will have a much easier time answering questions without constantly switching their attention. This leads to more detailed answers and ensures you receive accurate feedback on individual aspects of your idea. So, group related questions together to optimize your survey's performance.

3. INCLUDE LIKERT SCALES

Utilizing Likert scales in your surveys can significantly enhance the consistency of the collected data. Respondents are asked to rank their answers on a five-point or seven-point scale, ranging from "strongly agree" to "strongly disagree." This simple yet effective method simplifies the analysis process, making it easier to derive insights from the data. Additionally, using popular feedback collection tools such as the ones offered by HubSpot[3],

3 https://www.hubspot.com/products/service/customer-feedback

you can automate the reporting process and save time and re-sources for your team. With the familiarity and ease of use of Likert scales, your survey can become more user-friendly and generate better response rates.

4. USE VISUALS FOR ANSWERS

To get accurate feedback on a visual concept, it is vital to use images instead of relying on text. For instance, if you are conducting a survey to test new packaging designs, displaying their images and then asking participants to choose their preferred one is the best way to get unbiased and structured feedback. This approach enables you to gather consistent feedback and make confident decisions based on the results.

5. INCORPORATE DEMOGRAPHIC QUESTIONS

To ensure the success of your survey, it is crucial to identify the participants and confirm if they match your target market. Negative feedback from a participant does not necessarily mean that your concept is bad. It is possible that the participant is not part of your target group and is not interested in your product. Therefore, you must include demographic questions in your survey to determine the likelihood of your idea being successful among your intended consumer base.

To obtain accurate demographic information, you can ask questions such as:

- What is your age?
- What is your gender identity?
- What is your ethnicity?
- Where do you live?

- What is your highest level of education?
- Are you married?
- What is your annual household income?
- What is your current employment status?

By including these questions in your survey, you will be able to assess the potential success of your product among your target market.

CASE STUDY – CHOBANI

Chobani, the Greek yogurt company, invested heavily in concept testing to develop one of its most popular offerings - the Flip. Through rigorous experimentation, the company discovered that the best audience for the product was people who missed breakfast. Chobani created a product that was perfect for people on the go by catering to their needs. The company modified the packaging to ensure that mobile consumption was easy, thus creating the Chobani Flip.

Additionally, Chobani also used the concept testing process to test its ads. The company discovered that TV advertisements were the critical factor contributing to Flip's success in Australia. With this knowledge, Chobani created more campaigns that boosted overall sales in that region.

KEY TAKEAWAY

Your company's product can become a resounding success if you leverage the power of concept testing to make informed decisions that delight your target audience. Determine the appropriate tests, run them, and watch as you make better decisions that drive growth. However, remember that the success of concept testing is contingent on developing the right concept in the first place. With the right approach, you can confidently launch a product that meets the needs and wants of your customers.

CHAPTER 4

THE BUSINESS ANALYSIS PHASE

CARRYING OUT COMPREHENSIVE RESEARCH OF THE MARKET, BUSINESS GOALS, AND REQUIREMENTS.

Simply having an innovative idea is not enough to capture the market. You need a comprehensive plan to ensure success and profitability. That is why business analysis is so crucial in the process of developing new products. By conducting meticulous research on the market, business goals, and requirements, you can determine the feasibility of your idea and identify all possible challenges. With thorough business analysis, you can move forward with your idea, knowing you have a solid plan.

BUSINESS ANALYSIS – KEY PROCESSES AND RESULTS

With a comprehensive plan, you can navigate the process clearly and understand what to expect at every step.

1. GATHER RELEVANT INFORMATION

To ensure the success of your project, you must gather all the necessary information regarding the present situation in the field. This includes the latest industry trends and the most cutting-edge technologies used to develop products. Additionally, you need to pay close attention to external circumstances that can influence the outcome of your project, such as political, economic, socio-cultural, technological, and legal factors on both local and international scales. By being thorough in your research and analysis, you can confidently move forward with your project and maximize your chances of success.

POLITICAL FACTORS

Political factors are a crucial aspect that can significantly impact your business and the products you aim to develop. These factors encompass political stability, government policies, foreign trade policies, labor laws, tax policies, trade restrictions, etc. It is essential to stay updated with existing and future legislation to respond effectively and adjust your product development plan accordingly. To ensure your business stays ahead, ask yourself some critical questions such as:

- How can pending taxation changes or legislation impact your product's performance positively or negatively?
- Are there any trade restrictions on countries providing raw materials for your goods' development?

ECONOMIC FACTORS

Your product's performance and profitability are strongly influenced by economic factors such as exchange rates, economic growth, interest rates, inflation, and the disposable income of your target market. Understanding and effectively managing these factors can help ensure the success of your product in the market.

SOCIO-CULTURAL

Socio-cultural factors are the bedrock of shared attitudes and beliefs that form the fabric of a population. These factors are incredibly significant as they shape an individual's understanding of the consumer and the decisions they make. It is essential to consider a few things, such as the population's age profile and growth rate, which are subject to change. Additionally, you should ask yourself whether generational shifts in attitude will likely impact the product you are developing. By staying on top of these factors, you can navigate the market and create products that resonate with your target audience.

TECHNOLOGICAL FACTORS

You must be well aware of the fast-paced technological evolution and its impact on product development and marketing strategies. Anticipating the arrival of new technologies that could potentially render your product obsolete is a crucial aspect of staying ahead in the market.

LEGAL FACTORS

To ensure the success of your product, you should have a solid understanding of the legal factors that come into play. These factors include advertising standards, health and safety regulations, consumer laws and rights, product safety, and product labeling. Being well-versed in what is legal and what is not will help you to navigate this complex area easily. Even if you plan on launching your product globally, you can be assured that you are well-equipped to handle any legal challenges that come your way, as you have the knowledge to ensure compliance with the unique laws of every country.

2. DETERMINE THE STAKEHOLDERS

To ensure the success of your product, it is crucial to identify all the potential stakeholders. These are the individuals who have a vested interest in your product, either as potential consumers or decision-makers. For instance, if you are launching a new cereal brand for young children, your primary target audience would be the kids themselves. However, you must also recognize that the parents ultimately decide whether or not to buy the product. Therefore, they are a critical secondary audience you must keep in mind while developing your marketing and sales strategies.

3. IDENTIFY BUSINESS GOALS

To create a successful business plan, take a deep dive into the goals you want to achieve and the reasons why your product is needed. Once you clearly understand these goals, you and your team should work together to finalize them and create a comprehensive business plan that meets your requirements. Some essential goals you may want to focus on include acquiring new customers, increasing revenues and profit margins, and ensuring your existing customers are satisfied with your product or service. A robust business plan can set your company up for success and efficiently achieve your goals.

4. IDENTIFY AND ANALYZE YOUR OPTIONS

When carrying out a business analysis for a product, it is essential to generate multiple strategies to achieve the goals outlined earlier. After brainstorming, you and your team should shortlist and evaluate each option by considering the potential risks, impact, and cost-benefit ratio. With this approach, your business will be better equipped to make informed decisions and achieve success.

5. DEFINE THE PROJECT SCOPE

The scope of a project is critical in determining the deliverables that will be included in the process. As an expert in your field, understanding how each team functions and fits into the overarching process gives you the insight to determine what will be included in the project scope. Use the scope to break down deliverables into smaller parts and create a comprehensive list of tasks that need to be completed for each piece of work. This approach will ensure that every aspect of the project is accounted for and that the final deliverable meets or exceeds the expectations of all stakeholders.

6. CREATE A DETAILED OUTLINE

Here, you must create a well-defined delivery plan outlining your new product development schedule. This plan should include deadlines for key milestones such as the completion of the prototype and the product launch. To ensure success, it is crucial to establish achievable, practical, and realistic deadlines. It is also wise to build in some extra time to account for unforeseen circumstances. By taking these steps, you can confidently approach your new product development project and set yourself up for success.

7. DEFINE PROJECT REQUIREMENTS

The project requirements and scope are closely intertwined, and the requirements document serves as the ultimate guide for developing the product. It outlines:

- **Functional Requirements**: including the product's functions, features, processes, behaviors, and actions.
- **Non-functional Requirements**: such as scalability, accessibility, and compliance standards.

The product specifications document provides a comprehensive and in-depth overview of the product's objectives, goals, and functionality, leaving no room for ambiguity or uncertainty. With these documents, you can move forward with the development process, knowing you have a clear roadmap.

Based on your thorough business analysis conducted with the help of experienced specialists, you can gain a precise understanding of the product's economic viability, cost, competition, and demand. While the duration of this process depends entirely on the product's complexity and the approach used, your team's expertise and experience will allow you to carry out this analysis efficiently.

IMPORTANCE OF CARRYING OUT BUSINESS ANALYSIS IN NEW PRODUCT DEVELOPMENT

Based on the earlier discussion, it is imperative to conduct a thorough business analysis for the success of a new product. We have identified five compelling reasons to support this stance.

1. CLARITY ON TECHNICAL REQUIREMENTS

By spending ample time defining your business objectives and needs clearly, you pave the way for greater clarity in technical requirements. As a result, the probability of being dissatisfied with the final product is drastically reduced.

2. ALLOWS YOU TO SAVE TIME

When product requirements are crystal clear, there is no need to spend time explaining to the product developers and engineers what you need them to modify. This ensures that you will not have to wait for days to get changes executed during the new product development process. With fewer changes to make, you can finalize the product faster and bring it to the shelves of the stores quickly, allowing you to start profiting from it sooner.

This is especially crucial for products that rely on the latest trends and technologies. In such situations, wasting time is not an option if you want your product to be unique and one-of-a-kind. So, having a clear vision and concise product requirements is the key to success.

3. REDUCE DEVELOPMENT COSTS

When the requirements are clearly established and minimal time is required for executing changes, you can save a significant amount on development costs and prevent unpredictable expenses, such as delaying your product launch, which could cost you a fortune. By doing so, you can stick to your initial budget and ensure the success of your product launch.

4. YOU ARE AWARE OF THE NEEDS YOUR PRODUCT HAS TO FULFIL

You can significantly reduce the risk of your business going bankrupt by possessing deep insights into your target market's needs and preferences. This information is crucial for devising and implementing successful marketing strategies that resonate with your audience and attract more customers. Armed with this knowledge, you can steer your business toward success.

5. ALLOWS FOR SEAMLESS COMMUNICATION

Developing a new product can be a seamless process when all parties involved, including testers, developers, project managers, and product owners, are in agreement about what needs to be done and what steps are required. Through comprehensive business analysis, even the tiniest details can be determined in advance, minimizing the likelihood of errors or misunderstandings during development. As a result, you can expect fewer unpleasant surprises and more predictable outcomes. With this level of preparation, you can be confident in the success of your new product development project.

KEY TAKEAWAY

By conducting a thorough business analysis, you can clearly define the technical requirements for all stakeholders involved. This saves precious time, energy, and resources and ensures that the end product is top-notch quality and resonates well with the target audience. In short, business analysis is an indispensable tool to pave the way for a successful venture.

CHAPTER 5

PROTOTYPING

DEVELOPING A SAMPLE OF THE FINISHED PRODUCT TO SHARE WITH KEY STAKEHOLDERS.

In theory, many things can seem promising. However, the true challenge lies in ensuring that your product succeeds in the real world at a price point that consumers can easily afford. Finding the perfect formula for the market might require experimentation with different materials and combinations. But, with determination and hard work, you can make it happen.

You must identify and address potential problems as early as possible to succeed. The last thing you want is to waste time and money on a product that will not work for any reason. That is why thorough testing and proper market research with a well-functioning prototype are crucial. Doing so will give you the most precise and accurate information to advance your launch.

Remember, the prototype stage is the best time to identify and rectify faults. So, do not rush the launch without thoroughly testing your choices. With a solid plan, you can ensure that your product succeeds.

WHAT IS PROTOTYPING?

The term prototype finds its roots in the Greek word prōtos, which means first, and tupos, meaning figure or the defining feature of something. This implies that it represents an early effort to visualize all or part of a new product idea.

Technopedia[4] says, "A prototype is an example that serves as a basis for future models. Prototyping allows designers to research new alternatives and test the existing design to confirm a product's functionality before production."

Recently, prototyping has gained immense attention in product development research communities. It has become essential in various product and business development domains, especially with the rising interest in adopting Design Thinking.

Prototype testing is one of the most rewarding stages in developing new products. By creating a prototype of your product, you can bring your product idea to life for the first time and test it with a sample of your target market. Market testing your prototype will help you prepare your product for market entry and make any necessary improvements.

It is essential to understand that prototyping is not limited to developing a tangible mockup. It involves a proof of concept using DIY materials combined with off-the-shelf hardware or a completely functional product made with precision-crafted components.

IMPORTANCE OF PROTOTYPING IN NEW PRODUCT DEVELOPMENT

Starting with the importance of prototyping, I always create and share a draft of my work with my teammates while writing a chapter on any topic. By leveraging our collective knowledge and expertise, we can identify potential gaps and areas needing

4 https://www.techopedia.com/definition/678/prototype

improvement. This not only allows me to receive actionable feedback but also ensures that the final version of the chapter is more detailed and well-rounded, benefiting from the contributions of multiple people. As a result, I am confident in the quality of my work and can deliver the best version to my readers.

1. IMPROVED UNDERSTANDING OF THE DESIGN INTENTION

Prototyping is essential in product design as it provides a solid visual representation of the end product. More importantly, it allows the design team to understand better the design goals, the target audience, and the reasons behind the design choices. By prototyping, your team can create products that meet your customers' needs and exceed their expectations.

2. ALLOW YOU TO TEST AND REFINE THE FUNCTIONALITY OF YOUR PRODUCT DESIGN

Prototyping is an essential step in product development that enables you to test and validate your ideas. It is expected to overlook design flaws during the initial concept development and testing stages. However, prototyping provides a 3D model of your product, which uncovers potential design issues that could have gone unnoticed. This process allows you to make necessary adjustments and modifications to your product, ensuring it performs impeccably according to your expectations.

3. PROVIDES QUALITY ASSURANCE

It is a fact that not all products are created equally. If you have ever purchased a low-priced product online and had it malfunction or break after just a few uses, you know the frustration and disappointment that comes with it. But when you create a new product, you do not want to settle for anything less than the best. That is where quality assurance comes in – it gives you the confidence that your product is free from defects or problems and is ideally suited for regular use. With a prototype, you can ensure that your product is of the highest quality before it goes into mass production, giving you the peace of mind to take your business to the next level.

4. PROMPT FEEDBACK

Receiving feedback is an indispensable part of the product-building process. Prototyping helps you collect reviews at every step of creating your product, whether adding new features or tweaking existing ones. Analyze what works for your target audience and what does not. Define your goals unambiguously with management teams, team members, internal and external stakeholders, and arrive at the most optimal decision.

5. ESTIMATE THE COST OF PRODUCTION

Suppose you plan to present your product idea to potential investors or business partners. In that case, having all the necessary data to understand your constraints, such as cost and time, is crucial. Having a prototype can provide your engineers with a realistic estimate of the materials needed for production, and it also enables your accounting department to calculate the per-unit cost for manufacturing accurately. Ultimately, you will need to cover the production costs, and having an initial prototype can provide you with valuable information on materials and costs that you would not be able to obtain otherwise. With a prototype in hand, you can approach your investors and partners with greater confidence, knowing you have a solid understanding of the costs and materials required to bring your product to market.

6. ASSESSMENT OF PERFORMANCE ON THE MATERIALS USED

When creating a product, it is common to have primary specifications that include using a specific material to keep costs low. However, after making a prototype, it is crucial to evaluate the product's performance and consider if a more expensive material could enhance its performance enough to justify the higher expense. By trusting in your decision-making, you can ensure that your product is of the highest quality and meets your customers' needs.

7. SAVES COST AND TIME

Making changes towards the end can cause radical restructuring, leading to more rework and speculation. However, with a prototype, you can make the necessary changes early in the product development process, as no significant effort or investment has gone into creating the entire product. This approach enables you to accomplish your goals more quickly.

8. ATTRACTS INVESTORS

When meeting with potential investors, having a product prototype is imperative to ensure that you are taken seriously. In fact, a prototype is what distinguishes a mere idea from a computer-generated image or a simple sketch. With a prototype, you can easily showcase the real-life value of your idea without the fear of being caught off-guard when investors ask about its functionality. By having a prototype, you demonstrate that you are a serious professional with a well-thought-out project idea that is practical and ready to launch in the market.

9. VALIDATE YOUR IDEA BEFORE FINALIZATION

You can engage in multiple discussions and iterations through prototyping until you reach the final development stage. This iterative process gives you the assurance and conviction to create precisely what your consumers demand.

10. BENEFITS ALL DEPARTMENTS OF YOUR ORGANIZATION

Having a prototype is undoubtedly advantageous for the product development or engineering team. However, it is equally important that other relevant departments within your organization, such as marketing and sales, have a complete understanding of the product. This will enable them to create effective campaigns and sales pitches that accurately portray the product's value proposition. A prototype is the most valuable asset for such purposes, providing greater confidence in the product's potential success than mere sketches or drawings could ever offer.

11. CONSUMER RESEARCH AND TESTING

In today's world, consumers are the ones who hold power. Hence, it is crucial to identify your potential customers and obtain feedback to cater to their needs. Prototyping is a highly effective method to achieve this goal. The primary objective of developing a prototype is to conduct user testing, which provides valuable insights into the usefulness and usability of your product to the end consumer. Through user testing, you can gather insights and feedback on how real consumers would use your product and what improvements you can make to fulfill their requirements. With this approach, you can ensure your product will meet the needs and expectations of your target audience.

12. IDENTIFY THE MOST EFFICIENT MANUFACTURING METHOD

During the ideation and concept designing phase, it is expected to have a predetermined manufacturing process in mind for your product. However, creating a top-notch prototype can open up new possibilities and more efficient methods you may not have considered before. This can lead to a higher quality product and greater efficiency in the manufacturing process.

13. RESOLVE INTERNAL DISAGREEMENTS

Realizing and bringing your idea to a retail store requires significant organizational resources. However, disagreements among contributors or departments during the product development process can be a common barrier to success. A prototype can effectively settle arguments between designers, engineers, and other departments by providing a tangible example of how the product works. As a result, your team can set aside their differences and focus on optimizing the design to achieve the best possible outcome.

PROTOTYPING APPROACHES

Prototyping is a crucial phase in product development. With many prototyping approaches, selecting the one that fits your product's resources and time constraints is imperative. By choosing the right prototyping approach, you can deliver a successful product.

1. LOW FIDELITY PROTOTYPING APPROACH

Low-fidelity prototypes are an essential tool for any development team in the early stages of the product design process. These paper prototypes allow for rapid changes and iterations as the process advances, providing a fast and flexible way to refine the product. With a focus on the method rather than the final look, low-fidelity prototypes enable developers and designers to be more open to user feedback, making creating a product that meets their needs easier.

Using low-fidelity prototypes, team members and target market users can comprehensively understand the product and its features. However, as the product's complexity increases, it may become challenging to sustain low-fidelity prototypes into later stages of development. Therefore, while paper prototypes are an effective tool for early design, they may not be sufficient to sustain the necessary depth of design required for a more complex product.

2. MEDIUM FIDELITY PROTOTYPING APPROACH

Medium fidelity prototyping is an ideal approach to product development, as it allows you to create a realistic and functional product based on user scenarios and storyboards. This method is most appropriate for the intermediate stages of development as you move from low to high-fidelity designs.

3. HIGH FIDELITY PROTOTYPING APPROACH

Many people tend to confuse high fidelity with the final product, as they bear a striking resemblance to the actual final product. It is a fact that high-fidelity products are the best way to provide a highly realistic and practical experience of the original product. Although it may be a time-consuming and expensive process, the end result is worth it. High-fidelity products instill confidence in customers and leave a lasting positive impression, making them an ideal choice for businesses to showcase their products.

TIPS FOR EFFECTIVE PRODUCT PROTOTYPING

To ensure a successful product launch, it is crucial to prioritize prototyping and pay attention to the following tips. Invest adequate time and resources in this vital stage, and leverage your team's expertise to refine and optimize your product. With careful planning and execution, you can confidently bring your new product to market.

1. ASSIGN THE TASK TO SOMEONE

Identify a team member with strong project management skills and entrust them with coordinating and overseeing the product development and delivery process. Collaborate with your product development manager to establish a practical and well-informed schedule and project plan encompassing all the necessary steps to create a prototype and conduct market testing. Doing so can ensure your product development project's successful and timely completion.

2. CONSULT WITH PRODUCT DEVELOPMENT SPECIALISTS

Hiring product development experts can be a game-changer for your business. Their expertise can help you streamline the prototyping process and avoid costly mistakes in the long run. You can commission specialized consultants in product design and engineering, such as industrial or graphic designers, product quality consultants, product engineers, and computer-aided design (CAD) experts, who can provide invaluable assistance with prototyping. With their help, you can take your product development to the next level.

3. COMMISSION A PROTOTYPE OF YOUR PRODUCT

Developing a prototype is the key to determining the viability of your invention or idea. It provides you with all the necessary information to create your new product, identify defects or flaws in your design, and move forward with your product's branding, packaging, advertising, and marketing. By testing the look and feel of your product on sample segments of your target audience, you can be confident that you are creating a product that is tailor-made for your customers. It is essential to bring in technical expertise to guide you through this stage, especially if you don't have prior experience in product development. With the proper support, you can be confident that your prototype will set you on the path to success.

4. PUT THE PROTOTYPE TO TEST

As you put your prototype into use, it is essential to have confidence in its capabilities in the real-world scenarios it will encounter. To do this, it is crucial to identify the key features your customers require and subject them to rigorous testing to ensure their effectiveness. By repeatedly testing these characteristics, you can be confident that your product will meet your customers' needs.

5. CONDUCT FOCUS GROUPS

To ensure the success of your product, it is recommended that you hire a market research agency to conduct a comprehensive focus group, allowing you to measure and gauge the response of your target audience accurately. You must conduct in-depth interviews with your customers and present your prototype to a large number of individuals to gain valuable insights and ensure the success of your product.

6. MAKE NECESSARY MODIFICATIONS

Utilize the feedback gathered from focus groups and interviews to identify areas for potential improvement in your product. Take action and make modifications that will enhance your product's chances of success. Test the updated prototype under specific and targeted conditions to evaluate whether the changes have a positive impact. Consider conducting a follow-up focus group with the same participants to gauge their responses and determine if any noteworthy changes have been made. With this approach, you can increase your confidence in the product's potential for success.

7. TEST YOUR PROTOTYPE IN YOUR INDUSTRY

Attending consumer or trade expos and other industry events can be valuable to gain confidence in your product prototype. It allows you to showcase your product, create awareness, and receive constructive feedback. Additionally, it enables you to identify interested customer segments likely to attend your product launch or place advance orders, assuring you to take your product to the next level.

KEY TAKEAWAY

Prototyping offers numerous advantages throughout the various stages of bringing a new product to the market. If you want to accelerate your latest product opportunity and ensure its success, partnering with industry experts is the way to go. Innovolo[5] is an award-winning product design firm that provides end-to-end facilitation for your new product development. With their professional management of the vital steps of your product development process, you can be confident that your product will be a big success.

Moreover, if financing is a significant challenge for your product development process, companies like Innovolo can help. They provide comprehensive prototyping services and offer funding options for businesses lacking sufficient finances through various broker deals. With such companies by your side, you can navigate the complex world of product development and achieve your business goals.

5 https://innovolo-group.com/

CHAPTER 6

SOURCING FOR PRODUCT PRODUCTION

PUTTING TOGETHER A PLAN FOR VENDORS, MATERIALS, AND OTHER RESOURCES NEEDED TO TURN THE SUCCESSFUL PROTOTYPE INTO A MASS-MARKET PRODUCT.

Once you have a product prototype that meets your satisfaction, it is time to take the next step and start building your supply chain. This involves identifying potential suppliers, manufacturers, and partners you can rely on for large-scale production. At this stage, you should consider all aspects of your supply chain, including shipping, storage, and warehousing.

In Shoe Dog, Phil Knight - the founder of Nike - emphasizes the importance of expanding your supply chain network. Finding multiple suppliers for the materials you need, along with several potential manufacturers, will help you compare costs and develop a backup plan in case one does not work out. With several options, you can secure your business long-term and take your product to market.

SOURCING MATERIALS FOR YOUR PRODUCT

Building a product from scratch is an ambitious undertaking that requires careful consideration of all aspects, including sourcing suitable materials. While it can be challenging, with the right approach and mindset, you can navigate the process and find the best suppliers for your product. In this guide, you will discover the nine essential steps to help you easily source suitable materials and bring your product idea to life.

1. CONDUCT RESEARCH

Finding the right supplier for your product is crucial for its success. Your chosen supplier can substantially impact your product's quality, cost, packaging, and shipping. Fortunately, numerous tools are available to help you identify and select the best suppliers.

- **Alibaba**

Alibaba[6] links you with Chinese suppliers. It is a top-notch platform to consider. Not only can you find existing products quickly, but you can also leverage Alibaba to create customized products by directly contacting suppliers. Simply search for the materials you require and choose from numerous suppliers. With Alibaba's powerful filtering system, you can narrow your search results based on various criteria, including certifications like SA8000 certification, which guarantees a humanitarian working environment. So, rest assured that you will find a supplier who shares your organizational values.

- **Online Directories**

Free online directories can be a highly effective tool when searching for suppliers. With access to information on thousands of suppliers, wholesalers, and manufacturers, these directories can be game-changers. Here are some of the top overseas and domestic suppliers you should consider.

---

6 https://www.alibaba.com/

ONLINE DOMESTIC & OVERSEAS DIRECTORIES

- Kompass[7]
- MFG[8]
- Makers Row[9]
- National Association of Manufacturers Member List[10]
- ThomasNet[11]
- Sourcify[12]
- AliExpress[13]
- Oberlo[14]
- Indiamart[15]

- **Google**

Finding suppliers online has never been easier with Google. With just a few clicks, you can access the top search results and get what you are looking for. However, some suppliers have failed to keep up with Google's changing algorithms. Their websites are outdated, lack information, and are not optimized for search engines.

Fortunately, there are ways to use Google to your advantage. Do not be afraid to venture beyond the first page of search results and use various search phrases. Terms like "distributor," "wholesale," and "wholesaler" can be used interchangeably, so it is vital to search for all of them. With these tips, you can find

7 http://www.kompass.com/selectcountry/
8 http://www.mfg.com/
9 https://makersrow.com/
10 https://www.nam.org/workforce-solutions/directory/
11 http://www.thomasnet.com/
12 http://www.trysourcify.com/
13 http://www.aliexpress.com/
14 https://www.shopify.com/oberlo
15 http://www.indiamart.com/

suitable suppliers for your needs.

- **Referrals**

When finding the best leads, referrals are often the way to go. Reach out to your professional network and ask for their recommendations. Do not be troubled to connect with individuals who have succeeded in your desired field and ask them to share their contacts. And even if you encounter suppliers who are not a perfect fit, do not hesitate to ask for their guidance. As industry insiders, they likely have valuable connections and insights that can lead you to a better match. Make the most out of your networking efforts.

2. REACH OUT AND GET INFORMATION

Once you have a list of potential suppliers, it is time to request quotations. Do not settle for just one quote; aim for at least five from different suppliers. The key here is to compare and choose the best option. Although the cost is a significant factor, it should not be the only one to consider. Before you request the quotes, make sure you have answers to the following questions that will help you make an informed decision:

- **Do they take custom orders?** Check if the manufacturer or supplier can develop the product you need. Do they possess the resources for it? The skills?
- **What are their lead times?** How much time will it take to manufacture and send the products? You do not want to partner with a supplier who takes an unreasonable amount of time to ship your product. Additionally, if a product goes out of stock, you should never leave your customers waiting

months to receive their order. Work with reliable suppliers who can deliver goods promptly and ensure your clients are satisfied with their purchase experience.

- **What are the shipping costs?** Shipping constitutes a large percentage of your company's expenditures. Ensure you are well-versed with suppliers' shipping costs to assess how they will influence your revenues and profits.

- **What are the minimum order quantities?** Avoid starting with this question, as this will give the impression that you are an amateur and discourage suppliers from working with you. Nevertheless, you should know the minimum quantity of items you need to order before they start manufacturing your product. There is a high negotiation margin here.

- **What is the cost per unit?** When discussing minimum order quantities, you should also try to negotiate the cost per unit. The bigger your order, the lower your cost per unit should be.

- **Will they give you exclusivity?** Tooling (i.e., you purchase a tool for the suppliers to manufacture your goods) is involved in several situations. If so, you must ensure the supplier does not allow others to use it. You can even ask for market, territorial, or complete exclusivity.

- **Are there going to be setup fees?** Suppliers sometimes charge you a fee to ready the machinery needed to manufacture your products.

- **What is their policy for defects?** Determine who bears the cost for defective or incorrect goods. Additionally, find out who pays for the duties and shipping costs.

- **Is the supplier ethical and sustainable?** Get information regarding the working conditions of the factory and see how they influence the employees and the environment.

3. NEGOTIATE MINIMUM ORDER QUANTITIES

If you are new to the world of suppliers and minimum order requirements, also known as MOQs, do not worry. It is common for suppliers to ask for a commitment to purchase hundreds or thousands of pieces for your first order, depending on the product and manufacturer. However, remember that MOQs are usually negotiable, so do not hesitate to negotiate. Before you start negotiating, understand why the supplier set an MOQ in the first place. Is it because the product requires significant upfront work or because they prefer working with large-scale buyers? By familiarizing yourself with the reasons behind the MOQ, you can better understand their position and propose the best counteroffer.

4. DISCUSS TERMS OF PAYMENTS

When dealing with suppliers as a new product developer or business owner, Be aware that some suppliers may request full payment upfront. As inventory can be a significant cost for your business, it is essential to inquire about payment terms for future orders.

It is common for suppliers to receive numerous email quotation requests from uninterested or unreliable buyers who have not done their research. As a result, it is not uncommon for many suppliers to overlook or ignore certain emails.

To ensure you receive a response, avoid certain pitfalls when emailing suppliers for the first time. By being clear and concise in your message, doing your research, and presenting yourself as a serious and professional buyer, you can increase the likelihood of receiving a response from potential suppliers.

- **Lengthy emails:** When contacting a potential supplier, exude confidence and clarity in your first email. You do not need to provide an extensive background of your company or personal story. Instead, evaluate the potential fit between your needs and their capabilities. Provide the most valuable information to suppliers, such as the product details and specifications, to showcase your knowledge and expertise. Doing so will establish yourself as a confident and competent buyer, setting the tone for a successful business relationship.

- **Asking too much information:** To ensure you get the most out of your supplier, knowing what to ask when requesting quotations is important. While asking about pricing for various quantities is essential, it is equally important to avoid overwhelming the supplier with too many details or requests. You can determine whether the supplier fits your needs by asking only what you need to know.

Negotiating payment terms with manufacturing suppliers is standard practice, and the best suppliers are always open to it. If a supplier asks for full payment before shipping, it is a major red flag. However, you can always negotiate a deal that works for both parties. For example, you can propose paying 50 percent upfront and the remaining 50 percent upon receiving the shipment. Remember, you have the power to negotiate and find a payment plan that works best for you.

5. COMMUNICATE WITH SUPPLIERS

If you are just starting out, you might not have a manufacturing manager to communicate with the supplier, so you will have to speak directly to the suppliers. There are three practical ways to do this – through:

- Email
- Video call
- Chat app

Keep in mind that you should only work with suppliers who are responsive and eager to partner with you. If you encounter a supplier who does not respond to your emails and requests, it is best to look elsewhere. Remember, you deserve to work with suppliers who value your business and are committed to helping you succeed.

6. CONVEY YOUR DESIGN REQUIREMENTS

After speaking to a potential supplier, inquire about their capabilities to develop your design. While some suppliers offer product development services with 3D modeling and prototyping, it can be costly. However, you can effectively convey your design ideas through:

1. Instructions
2. Sketches
3. Reference images

Do not be discouraged if your supplier does not offer design services - you can easily find freelancers on Upwork[16] or Fiverr[17]

16 https://www.upwork.com/
17 https://www.fiverr.com/

who specialize in:

- CAD
- Product design
- Industrial design

Consider collaborating with a local designer to create customized molds and prototypes for a more cost-effective solution. You can easily navigate the development process by taking charge of your design needs.

7. PLACE AN ORDER FOR SAMPLES

Always secure samples for testing before proceeding to production and placing a full order. Once you have tested and approved the samples, sign and date them and keep two to three for your records. These are your control samples and serve as forensic evidence of the quality and uniformity of the products you expect to receive.

For example, if a supplier delivers an order with the wrong sizes, you can refer to your control sample to rectify the situation. This ensures you receive the agreed-upon items and prevents confusion or mistakes.

8. CARRY ANOTHER ROUND OF NEGOTIATIONS

When dealing with suppliers, negotiate effectively. From the moment you receive a sample to placing the final order, you can discuss things like MOQ and payment terms. However, keep in mind the supplier's perspective and not just focus on getting the lowest price possible. The ultimate goal should be establishing a mutually beneficial long-term relationship rather than exploiting the supplier for short-term gain. With a sound negotiation strategy, you can create a strong partnership that will benefit both parties for years.

KEY TAKEAWAY

Finding suitable suppliers can be challenging but essential to creating and launching a successful product. Choosing the right supplier can make all the difference in your product's success. It may seem daunting, but with perseverance and patience, you will find the perfect supplier to meet all your requirements. So do not get discouraged by roadblocks and dead ends. Keep pushing forward, and you will eventually find the ideal supplier for your new product.

CHAPTER 7

COSTING AND PRICING STRATEGIES FOR NEW PRODUCTS

DOCUMENTING ALL OF THE COSTS REQUIRED TO BRING THE PRODUCT TO MARKET.

Setting the right price for your new product is crucial and must be approached with facts and data, not guesswork. The price you establish for your product can either make or break your company's financial objectives, regardless of what product you are creating. A comprehensive pricing strategy is imperative when you want your consumers to purchase while maintaining lucrative profits.

While there is no one answer for your product price, remember that customers will only pick products that offer them the best value for money. Therefore, it is essential to determine the actual value of what you are selling, apart from manufacturing costs. With the appropriate pricing strategy, you can account for all the factors influencing a shopper's willingness to purchase.

Approach pricing with a well-researched strategy. Leaving it to guesswork can be a costly mistake. Take the time to understand the market, your competitors, and your target audience to set a price point that reflects the actual value of your product.

WHAT IS A PRICING STRATEGY?

Determining the right pricing strategy is crucial for any business owner or company to maximize profits. It involves various techniques, including calculations, market research, and consumer insights. While some business managers opt for simple approaches like established markups (also referred to as cost-plus pricing) or manufacturer-suggested retail prices (MSRPs), the most effective pricing strategy considers market conditions and other critical determinants of consumer behavior. With the right approach, you can set the optimal price for your product and achieve your business goals.

WHY DO YOU NEED TO HAVE A PRICING STRATEGY?

As e-commerce evolves, buyers have gained the power to easily compare prices, making it the second most helpful advantage of buying online. To stay ahead of the competition, you need a robust pricing strategy to help you fulfill your customers' expectations while giving you a competitive edge. With a well-planned pricing strategy, you can make informed decisions that align with your target market's preferences and your competitors' offerings. This will allow you to acquire even the most price-sensitive buyers, giving you a significant advantage in the market.

When combined with an excellent marketing strategy, your pricing strategy can help you enhance the perceived value of your products, boosting your brand's reputation and customer loyalty. So, invest time and effort in developing a solid pricing strategy to help you achieve your business goals and stand out in the market.

TYPES OF PRICING STRATEGIES

There are many pricing strategies available that can be utilized to price your new product. This section will examine fourteen pricing strategies, allowing you to understand their unique characteristics and make informed pricing decisions.

1. COST-PLUS PRICING STRATEGY

A cost-plus pricing strategy, also known as a Profit Markup strategy, is a highly effective method for businesses to determine the price of their products. It involves adding a markup to the production cost to achieve a specific profit margin. This pricing strategy is widely used by retailers and businesses, especially those that sell physical goods. However, it may not be suitable for companies that offer services.

To use this pricing strategy, you need to:

Step 1: Calculate your production cost.

Step 2: Decide on a profit per sale.

Step 3: Add a fixed percentage to the production cost.

For example, if you are selling a phone case that costs $15 to manufacture and want to achieve a 100% price markup, you would sell it for $30.

Overall, the cost-plus pricing method is a simple and effective way for businesses to set prices and achieve their desired profit margins. By using this strategy, companies can ensure they are earning a fair profit on their products while remaining competitive in their market.

2. COMPETITIVE PRICING STRATEGY

Competitive pricing is a well-known strategy involving pricing your products based on competitors' prices. It is an intelligent way to determine the right price point for your product and stay ahead of the competition. By exploring and analyzing the existing market rates for the product niche you are getting into, you can set a benchmark for your pricing strategy that is both competitive and profitable.

The cost of your competitor's product or demand does not play a role in this strategy. Instead, the competitor's price point is a benchmark on which you base your pricing. In other words, you determine the price of your product based on what consumers are already willing to pay for what the competition is offering.

Businesses typically adopt this strategy in highly competitive markets, where even a slight price change can significantly impact consumer demand. For example, if your competition has priced toothpaste at $2.99, you can price your toothpaste slightly lower ($2.70), the same, or even somewhat higher ($3.10) than the benchmark. However, if you price your toothpaste way above $4.50, your customers may lose interest and switch to other products that match the benchmark price.

Competitive pricing is a smart way to stay ahead of the competition, regardless of the price you keep. Setting a competitive price benchmark can attract more customers and increase your market share, even in highly saturated markets. Therefore, it is a proven pricing strategy for businesses to adopt to achieve long-term success and profitability.

3. FREEMIUM PRICING STRATEGY

The word freemium is an amalgamation of free + premium. Freemium is a proven pricing strategy widely used by businesses offering services such as software or applications. It allows consumers to try out a 'free trial' or a 'free basic version' of their product or service at an affordable rate. This strategy is designed to entice consumers to upgrade to the premium version of the product with its advanced features after testing its credibility.

The freemium pricing strategy is unsuitable for everyday household goods but has been a game-changer for software companies. It is not uncommon for software companies to offer a discounted rate on their product to give consumers a sneak peek into its performance.

The success of freemium pricing lies in building a bond of trust with the consumer base. Once the product's performance is established, consumers are more likely to pay the full price for the premium version of the product. Many software applications, such as Spotify, Netflix, and Avast, have leveraged this pricing model to their advantage.

In brief, the freemium pricing model mirrors the perceived value of the product that the company is offering, and it has proved to be a successful strategy in building a loyal customer base.

4. DYNAMIC PRICING STRATEGY

A Dynamic Pricing Strategy is undoubtedly one of the most flexible pricing strategies businesses implement to sell their products. It is also commonly known as demand or surge pricing, where prices fluctuate based on customer or market demand.

This strategy considers several factors influencing a customer's purchasing decision, such as market conditions, government sanctions, law and order, and many others. Airlines, venues, and hotels widely use this pricing strategy as it allows them to adjust the price according to the consumers' demand.

During the COVID-19 pandemic in 2020-21, airline prices fluctuated based on travel bans on different destinations. Several external factors determined whether or not it was safe to fly from one place to another, making it challenging for airlines to offer a fixed rate for their services.

5. PSYCHOLOGICAL PRICING STRATEGY

Psychological pricing is a powerful human psychology strategy to attract consumers toward a particular product. With its different sub-sections, such as the "**digit-effect**" or the "**buy one, get one**" offer, psychological pricing has proved to be highly effective in influencing consumers' buying decisions. In fact, most business models are built on human psychology, making them a crucial element in the success of any business.

The digit effect is a common pricing technique that you come across every day. It involves pricing a product at a price point that ends in '.99'. For example, a product priced at $49.99 instead of $50 can make consumers feel they are getting a better deal, even though the difference is only a cent. This is because the first digit being 100 units less, makes all the difference in the consumer's mind.

Similarly, the "buy one, get one free" offer is another psychological pricing technique that makes consumers feel like they are getting a good bargain. This can lead them to buy things even if they do not need them, just because they feel like they are getting a good deal. Some supermarkets and online stores also place expensive items next to their main focus products so consumers can see the price difference. This creates a perception of a good deal and encourages consumers to purchase.

Lastly, how you advertise the price is also a critical factor in psychological pricing. The font, placement, color, and advertisement quality directly impact consumers' buying decisions. By effectively understanding and using these techniques, businesses can significantly influence consumers' perception of their products and increase sales.

6. DISCOUNT PRICING STRATEGY

This pricing strategy is usually referred to as the high-low pricing strategy, a commonly used technique where the price of a product is reduced towards the end of its life cycle. This is typically seen in products sold at a higher price point when they are in demand but are put on sale or discounted when their popularity wanes. For instance, face masks that were once used as surgical masks in 2019 saw a surge in demand during the COVID-19 pandemic, prompting the production of various types of face masks by companies across the globe. However, as the pandemic subsided, face masks began to lose relevance, and their prices decreased to pre-pandemic levels.

Apart from socially relevant products like face masks, a discount pricing strategy is also used for fast-paced items like home décor, furniture, and fast-fashion products. Fashion stores, for instance, often put last season's styles on clearance as soon as the new collection is introduced. The discount pricing strategy is popular among consumers as they can take advantage of sales and discounts, especially during the holidays. Many consumers find it challenging to afford full-price products, and they tend to shop at their favorite stores during sales and discounts.

7. PENETRATION PRICING STRATEGY

A penetration pricing strategy is a powerful tool for businesses when entering the market. It involves setting exceptionally low prices to attract consumers and steal revenue from competitors. The strategy encourages customers to try new products, and businesses can cement their position before gradually increasing their prices to meet the market rate.

For example, imagine a wheat manufacturer introducing a new line of bread products. If the market price for a loaf of bread is $1.50, the manufacturer can use a penetrative pricing method and price the new product at around $0.99. The result is a wave of new customers eager to try the product, which creates a strong consumer base for the business.

Although losing customers after prices return to normal is expected, the penetrative pricing strategy works best for new businesses. Customers who take a liking to the product become repeat purchasers, and the strategy also promotes purchasing higher-priced products from the same seller. Overall, the penetrative pricing strategy effectively allows businesses to establish themselves in the market and gain a competitive edge.

8. SKIMMING PRICING STRATEGY

A skimming pricing strategy is highly effective for pricing novelty items such as smartphones, gaming consoles, and other tech gadgets with a shorter life cycle. Products such as DVD players, which are no longer in demand, are available at a much lower price compared to all the other gadgets released in the market. Companies adopt the skimming strategy by charging a significantly higher price than the product's production cost to recover sunk expenses and advertising costs. Products that enter the market with price-skimming marketing strategies inevitably lose their relevance pretty quickly. However, companies are quick to adapt and lower the price until the product is discontinued.

9. BUNDLE PRICING STRATEGY

A company can use a bundle pricing strategy when offering two or more products together. This is an excellent option for creating a basket of complementary goods sold at a value price. For instance, a shortbread and jam collection pack that retails for $17.99, while individually, all products can total up to $21.99, is a good example of bundle pricing. By buying the bundle, the consumer can save approximately $4.

The bundle pricing strategy offers a significant advantage to the company as well. Suppose a consumer walks in to buy a pack of shortbreads worth $7.99 and decides to purchase the bundle deal instead. In that case, the company earns $10 more than intended. Although the company may make lower profits on the bundle, it increases customer satisfaction and, consequently, higher repeat purchase incidences.

Furthermore, the company can use this strategy to its advantage by selling its products in bundle and individual form. This gives the consumer the flexibility to choose the option that fits their needs while ensuring that the company can maximize its profits.

10. PREMIUM PRICING STRATEGY

A Premium Pricing Strategy, or luxury pricing, is a powerful tool for companies to promote a premium, high-end product image. This strategy involves pricing products at incredibly high rates that focus more on the perceived value of the good rather than its actual production cost. High-end designers and technology brands often adopt this pricing strategy to convey exclusivity and luxury to customers.

Customers are willing to pay exorbitant prices for such products because they believe they can gain the desired status and value. This is particularly true for designer brands like Prada, Calvin Klein, and Gucci. Most high-end apparel and technology brands boast of being rare and exclusive, attracting consumers who seek to stand out and appear unique.

However, this pricing strategy requires high brand awareness and a strong brand perception. Not every company can successfully implement this strategy. Only companies with a well-established and highly regarded brand can adopt this pricing strategy to impact consumers positively.

11. HOURLY PRICING STRATEGY

Businesses and industries that charge by the hour tend to use the hourly pricing strategy more frequently, as it offers a fair and transparent pricing model. Whether it is freelancers, consultants, or laborers, the hourly charge is now an expected norm. In some cases, even firms such as mechanics and machine-repair technicians offer services based on hourly pricing strategies due to the shift in the market.

This strategy allows workers to trade their time for money, and it usually functions on a fixed rate with additional charges for extra time spent.

Here is an example: if you hire an electrician who charges $20/hour and $7 for every additional 15 minutes, you will pay $34 for 90 minutes of work ($20+$7+$7=$34). With the hourly pricing strategy, the worker and the client can rest assured that they are getting a fair deal.

12. GEOGRAPHICAL PRICING STRATEGY

A Geographical Pricing Strategy is a powerful tool that businesses use to set prices based on the geographical location of their customers. This pricing strategy is particularly effective for products sold in multiple countries, as the cost of production and the price of the product can vary greatly depending on the location of the manufacturing facilities. For example, a well-known fashion brand like H&M produces products in various countries using different contractors and raw materials. As a result, the cost of producing a product in India may significantly differ from the cost of producing the same product in France.

13. VALUE-BASED PRICING STRATEGY

A Value-based Pricing Strategy is the most effective pricing approach as it is based on the consumer's viewpoint and perception of a product's value. It involves assessing how much a consumer is willing to pay for a particular product and setting the price accordingly. A product's utility and functionality may justify a higher price, but its perceived value can influence how much a company charges. Therefore, businesses must deeply understand their consumers' sentiments and personalities to set the appropriate prices. By adopting a value-based pricing strategy, brands can attract more customers and build customer loyalty, leading to increased profits.

14. PROJECT-BASED PRICING STRATEGY

The Project-Based Pricing approach is a superior pricing strategy that charges a flat rate for a specific service the company offers. This method focuses more on delivering high-quality project outcomes than tracking employee work hours.

Business service providers such as contractors and freelancers typically use project-based pricing as it aligns better with their skills and expertise. Companies prefer this pricing strategy for projects that demand exceptional quality, as hourly rates may not do justice to the complexity and effort involved.

WHICH PRICING STRATEGY SHOULD YOU USE?

When determining the best pricing strategy for your product, remember that pricing strategies are not set in stone and can change over time as your product progresses through its lifecycle. However, the introductory stage is often the most challenging. Nevertheless, once you decide to launch a new product, you will undoubtedly encounter difficulty setting a price for it. While businesses worldwide use several pricing strategies, it is essential to understand that not all of them may be suitable for your product. Your product is unique and different, so that a selective pricing strategy will work best for you.

When it comes to standard pricing for consumer goods, the most commonly used pricing strategies are Price Skimming and Market

Penetration. Let us examine them further:

As mentioned earlier, Price Skimming or Market Skimming Pricing is an excellent pricing strategy for new products. This strategy allows the company to set a high price for a product, enabling it to skim the maximum level of revenues from consumer segments willing to pay a premium price.

Once a business procures revenues from high-paying consumer segments, the company then lowers the price to skim maximum profit from the remaining consumer segments. As the pricing strategy progresses, the company may make fewer sales, but they are profitable.

Several companies that invent new products set high prices to gain revenues from the market. An excellent example is the new product pricing strategy used by the tech giant Apple Inc[18].

Tech Giant Apple Inc. uses Price Skimming for their infamous iPhones

Despite the relatively high price of the new iPhone upon launch, consumers were more than willing to pay just to own the latest technology. Apple successfully capitalized on this initial demand from early adopters to earn maximum profits before dropping prices to attract a broader range of consumers. Through this strategic approach, Apple was able to effectively target and skim off the maximum profit from multiple consumer segments in a relatively short period.

Remember that implementing a Price Skimming strategy for your new product may or may not be the smart way to go. It only works under certain conditions, such as a strong brand image,

18 http://www.apple.com/

high product quality, and favorable brand perception. Without these factors, your product may not be successful even with a high initial price.

Furthermore, the cost of producing a small number of products is not a good enough reason to justify a high initial price. Apple successfully charged a high price for their products because they were a relatively new technology in the market, which over-shadowed their production cost and gave them the advantage of charging a higher price.

Despite these factors, if you believe your product is worth a high initial price and a price-skimming strategy is for you, be aware of your competitors. Competitors can be disadvantaged even with a high initial price and good consumer behavior. Suppose a competitor enters the market by lowering the cost of the same product that you are offering. In that case, consumers will not take long to switch to the competitor's side. Hence, price skimming may not work.

On the other hand, if you opt for Market Penetration Pricing for your new product placement, you need to set a low price instead of setting a high initial price so that your new product can easily penetrate the market.

A low price on your new product will give you an advantage over your competitors so your brand can penetrate the market deeply. A business can sway a large number of buyers through a low price. However, keep in mind that you will have to forego profitability, at least in the beginning.

This does not mean you will not make any profits from your new product. You must understand that even though each sale may not be profitable, the high sales volume brought by market penetration can significantly reduce your costs. Once your cost of production decreases, you will begin to profit through your new product.

JAPANESE CONVENIENCE BRANDS: MARKET PENETRATION AT ITS BEST

Japanese convenience brands are a perfect example to illustrate the effectiveness of Market Penetration Pricing. The secret behind their tremendous success lies in their ability to introduce products at unbelievably low prices, attracting many customers. As a result, they manage to capture a significant market share because consumers are always looking for affordable everyday consumer goods. Despite the lower profit margin per sale, the high-volume sales always lead them toward a profitable outcome.

It is necessary to remember that no pricing strategy can work independently. Whether it is Market Penetration or Price Skimming, any product pricing strategy must meet certain conditions to be profitable.

FACTORS YOUR PRICING STRATEGIES SHOULD DEPEND ON:

Consider the following factors to ensure your pricing strategy is effective for the product you are trying to sell. Doing so lets you choose a pricing strategy that meets your objectives and maximizes your revenue potential.

COSTS

To devise an effective pricing strategy, thoroughly understand your financial situation. Take the time to calculate your business costs and expenses before making any decisions. This way, you will have the necessary knowledge to set prices to ensure your business's profitability and success.

CONSUMER DEMAND

Based on my experience and observations, I recommend closely examining your product offering and its consumer demand. Understanding your customers' needs and pricing preferences is crucial for a profitable business. Do not hesitate to pivot your market strategy to align with your customers' expectations if necessary. Doing so can position your business for long-term success and growth.

POSITIONING

You must assess your desired position in the marketplace. Determine whether your product is a luxurious, high-end brand or a fast-moving, affordable item.

COMPETITION

Your uniqueness is what distinguishes you from your competitors. Clearly understand your target audience's needs and always strive to exceed their expectations. Despite the competition, stand out as the preferred choice for your consumers. Establish your positioning in the marketplace, and continuously work towards maintaining your position. While your competitors may have their strengths, always look for ways to improve and innovate, ensuring your continued success.

PROFITABILITY

Focus on what you believe your product or service is worth rather than what others charge. Your offering can enrich your customers' lives, but your profit will enrich yours. Be assertive in your pricing strategy, and do not let the competition dictate your worth.

CHAPTER 8

MARKETING NEW PRODUCTS

DESIGNING AN INITIAL MARKETING STRATEGY FOR A NEW PRODUCT

This chapter will investigate the role of marketing strategies in promoting your FMCG product. Let us begin by exploring marketing strategies and why they are essential for your success.

WHAT IS A MARKETING STRATEGY, AND WHY DO WE NEED ONE?

Marketing strategies are essential for any business to maintain its position in the market and create a solid consumer base. A good marketing strategy connects consumers with the business and drives revenue. It helps businesses understand their market, target customers, and competitors, ultimately refining their approach for future growth.

A well-crafted marketing strategy allows businesses to create content or campaigns that resonate with their customers' needs and wants, resulting in increased sales and reliable results. On the other hand, a lack of understanding of the market and customers can lead to significant risks and consequences. Therefore, investing in strategic marketing planning is crucial for businesses to succeed.

Overall, a marketing strategy comprises the classic Four P's of Marketing: **Product**, **Price**, **Place**, and **Promotion**, is a revenue driver that can help businesses achieve their goals and create a solid future.

MARKETING STRATEGIES FOR NEW FMCG PRODUCTS

Successful brands across the globe implement a variety of marketing strategies to gain a competitive edge and achieve profitable outcomes. These strategies are:

1. PRODUCT FLANKING

Product flanking is undeniably one of the most widely used and effective marketing strategies companies use worldwide. The strategy involves introducing new products so that each consumer segment has a tailored variation that caters to their unique preferences in terms of size or product price. By offering diverse combinations of new products at different prices, companies can tap into various market opportunities and capture different market segments. For instance, offering shampoo or detergent powder in multiple sizes, such as economy packs, industrial-sized packaging, travel sizes, small tubes, etc., ensures that every consumer segment can find something to buy based on their purchasing power and needs.

2. BRAND EXTENSION

Brand extensions are a proven strategy for companies to capitalize on the success of an established brand. While launching a new brand can be time-consuming, extending an existing brand offers instant recognition and faster acceptance in the consumer market. This is especially true when a parent company launches smaller subsidiary companies that leverage the equity and popularity of the parent brand. With this approach, companies can confidently expand their reach and build upon their success.

3. MULTI-BRAND STRATEGY

The Multi-Brand Marketing Strategy is a powerful tool, born from the idea that no single brand can cater to the entire consumer market. A company can capture a higher market share by marketing two or more competing products. Each competing product can achieve its market share, covering as many segments as possible. While some segments may overlap, most market share is unique and based on the product's identity and brand image.

This marketing strategy enables a brand to occupy more space in supermarkets, cementing its position in the market and building a strong consumer base. A great example of this approach is Cadbury, which has several chocolate brands, including Dairy Milk, Buttons, and Crème Eggs, each catering to different market segments. With a Multi-Brand Marketing Strategy, a company can expand its reach and establish a dominant presence in the market.

4. PRODUCT LINE STRATEGY

A brand can significantly benefit by implementing a new product line strategy that offers consumers a one-stop-shop experience. With this approach, consumers do not need to spend time deciding what to buy, leading to a higher success rate for the business. A perfect example of this marketing strategy is Unilever, which has an extensive range of products that complement each other. For instance, someone looking for antibacterial soap can quickly discover a beauty soap under the same brand's name, resulting in more sales.

5. INNOVATION MARKETING STRATEGY

It is imperative to comprehend that FMCG products have a brief lifespan in the market. Therefore, a brand that consistently introduces innovations to its core products can significantly increase sales and foster stronger consumer relationships. Such innovations may include changes in consumer preferences, technological advancements, or even addressing customer complaints. By doing so, the brand can establish itself as a leader in the market, paving the way for long-term success.

6. NEW PRODUCT DEVELOPMENT

Introducing a new product can be a game-changer for any company looking to expand its customer base. By focusing on new product development, a company can tap into an untapped market and attract new customers, benefiting all their product lines. Companies that invest in innovation and constantly bring new products to market often succeed in fast-paced, ever-changing markets. They can stay relevant and meet their customers' evolving needs, leading to sustained growth and profitability.

7. PRODUCT LIFE CYCLE EXTENSION

To stay ahead of competitors, companies often need to extend the life cycle of their product line. When a product reaches its mature stage, adding value or innovation is crucial to keep it relevant and successful. While some companies may pull weaker products when market conditions change, it is not always the best strategy. A mature product with a strong reputation can still thrive with updates or a fresh look, often more cost-effective than developing and launching a replacement product. In short, extending a product's life cycle can be an innovative move for a company.

8. MARKET EXPANSION

Expanding a market for an existing fast-moving consumer good can be achieved in two ways: by increasing consumption or increasing customers. To tap into a larger market share and boost sales, a brand needs to successfully increase the usage rate of its products among consumers. However, for this strategy to work, a company needs to know its product's potential and how its usage and usefulness can be measured.

To establish a product more than what the market perceives, companies can introduce new ways to use the product and give it a new direction. This approach can persuade new consumers to purchase the product and even convince existing ones to consume it more frequently. By selling their products in different variations and educating their consumer base on how they can use the product more regularly to make their life better or easier, companies can achieve a higher market share for their products.

Any product that can be used in varied ways automatically has a higher market share over single-use products. With the right strategies and product positioning, companies can expand their market share and establish their products more successfully.

9. DISTRIBUTION NETWORK STRATEGY

A wide distribution channel is vital to turning an average product company into a market leader. The success of a product is mainly dependent on how efficient its distribution network is, regardless of its features and uses. Therefore, developing a concrete distribution strategy is decisive for tapping into different consumer segments and staying ahead of the competition. A product becomes more visible by reaching more locations, contributing to its hype and popularity. Without a strong distribution network, a product's other features, such as functionality, usage, and quality, are not enough to sustain its position in the market. Thus, it is necessary to establish a vast distribution network for your products.

While acquiring an existing distribution network is common for many companies to widen their distribution, collaboration with other businesses that can stock your product is also an excellent approach.

DIGITAL MARKETING STRATEGIES

In the previous section, we discussed traditional marketing strategies. However, businesses must incorporate modern digital marketing techniques to succeed in this digital age. Companies that have taken the time to build a robust digital brand image are already reaping the benefits of their efforts. With most people using phones and tablets as their primary source of information, it has become paramount for businesses to adopt digital marketing strategies to successfully launch a new product in the market. So, let us dive into digital marketing and explore strategies to help you launch your new product.

1. PRE-LAUNCH EXCITEMENT

To ensure a product's success among diverse consumer segments, a company must generate a buzz during its release. Pre-launch product excitement can be created well in advance or several months after the product arrives on the store shelves.

One of the most effective ways to create pre-launch anticipation is organizing giveaways, challenges, and contests. This tactic ignites excitement among the customers and motivates them to explore the new product's features. Creative and innovative launch ideas attract customers more than any other marketing technique.

In simpler terms, if a company's digital marketing strategy can make its product go viral through social media, it can create a robust customer base. Remember that a pre-launch buzz can significantly impact the future brand image of your product, as it has the power to establish itself in consumers' subconscious minds.

2. WEBSITE OPTIMIZATION

A well-optimized website is a highly effective tool for engaging consumers and showcasing your brand. It lets visitors easily explore your products, prices, and features, giving them the information they need to make informed purchasing decisions. Website optimization is essential to target consumers online and in the physical marketplace.

A fast, visually appealing, and highly functional website establishes a positive and professional image for your brand, which can go a long way in building consumer trust and loyalty. On the other hand, a poorly optimized website can be detrimental to your brand's reputation and credibility. Therefore, investing in a well-optimized website is a crucial step toward achieving your digital marketing goals and ensuring the success of your business.

3. ORGANIC VISIBILITY

You need to focus on your search engine optimization to achieve steady traffic to your website and gain an advantage over your competitors. Optimized content and increased organic visibility allow you to easily reach your target audience and showcase your new product. Using relevant keywords and meta descriptions can provide valuable information to your users and attract more organic traffic. So, do not miss out on the opportunity to build a solid consumer base and boost your online presence with effective search engine optimization.

4. EMAIL/TEXT MESSAGE MARKETING

Do not overlook email and text message marketing to ensure effective marketing efforts. These forms of communication offer a direct and reliable way to reach your target audience and can help build brand awareness and product interest. By creating a database of your clients based on demographics, previous purchases, or interests, you can create highly personalized messages that are more likely to capture their attention and motivate them to take action. With the right approach and strategy, email and text message marketing can be a powerful tool for growing your business and achieving your marketing goals.

5. CREATE ENGAGING CONTENT

To captivate consumers' attention, creating engaging and shareable content is imperative. But merely listing the features of a product will not make the cut. Instead, the focus should be on creating an image of how the consumers will feel after purchasing the product. Brands that sell a feeling rather than a product tend to do better because they directly target the emotions of their audience.

Apart from the traditional quotes and aesthetics, it is crucial to highlight how the product can make the consumer feel. For instance, if you are marketing a detergent, you should emphasize how using your brand will make the user feel hassle-free with fresh-smelling clothes at the end of each laundry load. By doing so, you can instill confidence in your consumers, which will help you stand out from the competition.

6. SEARCH FOR INFLUENCERS

To expand on the previous point about focusing on a feeling, it is noteworthy that the reason behind the success of influencers in today's market is their ability to market a feeling through their unique perspectives.

When consumers watch an influencer using a product in their personal space, they instinctively connect with the same positive emotions the influencer tries to convey.

Therefore, conducting thorough research on a handful of influencers who align with your product's image and bringing them on board to promote your offering is needed.

7. VIDEO MARKETING

Consumers have shifted towards visual content in recent years, making imagery more important than words. Digital video platforms have become the preferred medium, and marketers use influencer-driven video content to reach their target audience.

When it comes to online marketing and video-based content,

YouTube is the ultimate hub. Among the most popular types of videos are directly addressing the viewers' concerns. By doing so, businesses can create a more relatable image with the ability to connect with the audience on an emotional level.

Successful video marketing is all about storytelling, which reveals the human side of a brand and draws in consumers. A compelling story about a product or a business can be incredibly persuasive to convince customers to purchase. Customers can relate and imagine using it by showing how the product can solve their problems.

If you plan to market a product, consider doing so through a video. However, remember that consumers have short attention spans, so keep it short and simple. Your stories must be compelling enough to make a long-lasting impact on the consumer.

Do not be afraid to go all out with your marketing techniques. Although it may seem overwhelming initially, the rewards can be highly beneficial in the long and short run.

CHAPTER 9

DISTRIBUTION AND ROLL OUT

MAKING THE PRODUCT AVAILABLE FOR PURCHASE BY DISPERSING IT THROUGH THE MARKET

In this chapter, you will learn about the meaning of product distribution and various distribution methods and strategies that you can confidently utilize to optimize your product's reach and visibility in the market.

WHAT IS PRODUCT DISTRIBUTION?

Product distribution is a vital aspect of any business. It is the process through which a product reaches the final consumer, and it is crucial for manufacturers to create effective distribution channels to ensure their products reach the widest possible audience. By creating multiple channels, manufacturers can provide their customers with easy access, which is vital as consumers enjoy diversity and availability on different levels. Hence, businesses need to highlight a distribution process that allows for a good amount of sales and accessibility for the consumers. A poorly designed distribution process can lead to a potential failure, and manufacturers must ensure they cater to the majority of their consumer segments to avoid such mishaps.

WHAT ROLE DOES A DISTRIBUTION CHANNEL PLAY IN PRODUCT DISTRIBUTION?

A distribution channel is an essential tool that helps businesses to target and reach their customers. Creating a distribution path allows the products to flow through and reach the intended market easily. It is a crucial link between producers and end consumers, with intermediaries like wholesalers and retailers playing a vital role in the process.

While distribution channels offer several benefits, such as increasing sales and accessibility to the consumer, it is essential to remember that they also affect the product's prices. The positioning of distribution channels depends on several factors, as each has a different cost.

Ideally, a distribution channel should have a limited number of stops to reach the end consumer as quickly as possible—the more stops in between, the higher the product costs. An extended distribution channel can lead to increased transportation costs, broker fees, logistical requirements, storage, and other costs impacting the final product rate.

Larger businesses often tackle this issue through economies of scale, using maximum capacity in transportation and storage to offer their consumers the lowest rates possible. Smaller businesses that cannot afford this generally charge their customers a higher price. A well-planned distribution channel is a critical strategy to help businesses grow and succeed in the highly competitive market.

TYPES OF DISTRIBUTION CHANNELS

There are two main types of distribution channels used globally - direct and indirect. Allow me to give you a classic example:

Manufacturer – Wholesaler – Retailer – End Consumer

Manufacturer – Retailer – End Consumer

Manufacturer – End Consumer

DIRECT DISTRIBUTION CHANNELS

A direct distribution channel excludes intermediaries. This channel allows manufacturers or producers to sell their products directly to the end customer. This method is often used by manufacturers and producers of expensive, niche goods and perishable items to ensure that their products are delivered to the customer as fresh as possible. For instance, fresh produce stores or bakeries are great examples of businesses that benefit from direct distribution. If they were to switch to indirect distribution channels, the quality of their products would suffer, leading to a subpar experience for the consumer.

INDIRECT DISTRIBUTION CHANNELS

On the far end of the distribution spectrum lies the indirect distribution channel, which utilizes a range of intermediaries to facilitate the movement of the product from the manufacturer to the ultimate consumer. This type of distribution channel can be classified into three distinct categories:

ONE LEVEL CHANNEL

Manufacturer –Retailer – End Consumer

In a one-level channel, there is only one intermediary between the manufacturer and the end consumer, which makes it a straight-forward and efficient distribution channel. The product is sent to a retailer, such as a supermarket or an online store, before being sold to the end consumer. This type of channel is perfect for manufacturers of various products, including but not limited to furniture, clothing, and toys. The retailer purchases the product directly from the manufacturer and then sells it to the customers, making it a simple and effective distribution model.

TWO LEVEL CHANNEL

Manufacturer – Wholesaler – Retailer – End Consumer

A two-level distribution channel is an effective strategy that involves intermediaries like wholesalers and retailers between the manufacturer and the end consumer. In this channel, the wholesalers purchase goods in bulk from the producers and then divide them into smaller sections to sell them to different retailers. Finally, the retailers distribute the products to the end consumers. This approach is suitable for larger markets and long-lasting goods. However, it is inappropriate for perishable or expensive products requiring special handling and care. With two-level distribution channels, businesses can reach a wider audience and increase their sales by tapping into multiple retail outlets.

THREE LEVEL CHANNEL

Manufacturer – Agent – Wholesaler – Retailer – End Consumer

The three-level distribution channel resembles the two-level channel, comprising a wholesaler and a retailer. However, in a three-level channel, the manufacturer enlists the help of an agent to sell the goods. The agent facilitates the delivery of the products to the wholesaler, who then purchases them in bulk and distributes them amongst multiple retailers. This enables the end consumer to buy the product through various retailers.

As an intermediary in the three-level channel, the agent receives a commission based on the product distribution in different areas. The commission is decided through negotiations between the manufacturer and the agent based on the agent's job description and fulfillment. The three-level distribution channel is most suitable for high-demand products and a large target market nationwide.

HOW DO YOU DECIDE ON A DISTRIBUTION CHANNEL?

Choosing the right distribution channel is crucial for any manufacturer to achieve their sales targets. The selection of distribution channels solely depends on the type of product or service and the manufacturer's sales objectives. The distribution channels play a significant role in determining the success of a manufacturer's sales strategy, and therefore, it is essential to choose the optimal distribution method for your product. To ensure maximum profitability, generate a considerable amount of sales, and increase consumer reach, you must evaluate key factors such as:

- Market Characteristics
- Product Type
- Competitor Analysis
- Company Sector and type

These factors must be evaluated in detail to determine the ideal distribution method for your business.

WHAT ROLE DOES E-COMMERCE PLAY IN PRODUCT DISTRIBUTION?

E-commerce has experienced unprecedented growth in the last few decades, providing manufacturers and producers with a direct-to-consumer selling opportunity. Online marketplaces like Ali Express, Amazon, eBay, and Alibaba have become ideal platforms for manufacturers and producers to offer their products and services to consumers. The internet plays a crucial role as an intermediary in this modern-day distribution channel. Although tangible item delivery is still required, global delivery services like Uber and DHL are also integral to this distribution channel. Overall, it is safe to say that this modern-day distribution channel is thriving with efficiency.

ADVANTAGES OF A DISTRIBUTION CHANNEL

REDUCED COSTS

It is important to note that utilizing a distribution channel can significantly reduce costs and extend a company's geographical reach. While a company may be capable of distributing its product, this can result in a significant investment of time and resources. On the other hand, an existing distribution network is already equipped with the necessary resources and channels to maneuver the product from one place to another quickly. Therefore, it makes more sense for a producer or manufacturer to leverage these services, as doing so is cost-effective and ensures greater efficiency and effectiveness.

EFFICIENT MARKETING

Collaborating with intermediaries in a distribution channel is a proven strategy to maximize your product's marketing potential. Joint marketing or promotional campaigns can attract substantial traffic to retail outlets and supermarkets without requiring you to take on the entire burden of an advertising campaign. The goodwill and equity of distribution channel intermediaries can be leveraged to bring in their customers towards the manufacturer's products. This can significantly boost brand awareness and sales, giving you a competitive edge in the market.

EXPANDING TO A NEW TERRITORY

Choosing the right intermediary with extensive knowledge of the local area and a deep understanding of its customers can be a game changer for companies. With an effective distribution channel, a business can effortlessly expand into new territories and target new consumer segments. Wholesalers and retailers handle intricate details in the product distribution process that producers and manufacturers do not have to worry about. This includes building strong retailer and customer relationships, providing exceptional customer services, and managing the producer's product inventory.

LOGISTICAL SUPPORT

Wholesalers, distributors, and retailers are highly efficient in managing their stocks. They are experts in fulfilling daily orders promptly and have the necessary equipment to handle large shipments. Distributors and retailers strive to provide quick shipments, ensuring a seamless flow of products to the end consumer. As a result, producers and manufacturers are relieved of the responsibility of fulfilling shipments or dealing with any logistical errors.

EASY FEEDBACK

Placing a product at a specific supermarket or retailer can benefit manufacturers and producers. By doing so, they gain direct access to valuable customer feedback that can be used to enhance their products and improve overall performance.

FORMS OF PRODUCT DISTRIBUTION

The following table exemplifies various forms of product distribution commonly used by producers and manufacturers in the market:

DEALERSHIP NETWORK	Utilizing an established network of authorized dealerships, which may be independently owned, is a savvy business strategy. For example, car manufacturers may have their cars sold through existing dealerships.
SALES AGENT	Partnering with several experienced sales agents on a commission basis is a reliable way to sell products. For instance, property developers often work with real estate agents to sell properties.
VALUE ADDED RESELLER	Partnering with value-added resellers who can sell a product as a value addition to their product is a smart move for manufacturers. For example, a construction agency may partner with a solar panel provider to sell solar panels as an addition to their construction services.

DIRECT MARKETING	Direct marketing via television or print ads, providing a direct number for customers to call and purchase, is an excellent way to sell products. Telemarketing is one such example.
E-COMMERCE	Selling products through an exclusive website, with paid internet promotions and advertising, is a popular and effective way for businesses to reach customers online. Internet providers, for example, may choose to sell their services through their websites.
DIRECT MAIL	Sending catalogs or brochures via direct mail to existing or target customers is a tried-and-true marketing strategy. In return, consumers can purchase over the phone, online, or in-store.
PERSONAL SELLING	Selling directly to customers at social events or places is a powerful way to reach potential buyers. For example, a college consulting company may sell services directly to students at college counseling events and education.
RETAIL	Opening its chain of retail shops is a common strategy for manufacturers or producers to sell their products directly to customers. For example, a chocolate and sweets manufacturer may open its candy retail store.
RETAIL PARTNER	Working with several retail partners to get products on the market is a widespread business practice. For example, a toy company may provide its products to leading children's stores.
INTERNATIONAL PARTNERS	Opening retail stores in their home country and internationally is a smart strategy for businesses looking to expand their reach. For example, H&M has apparel stores in several countries worldwide.

WHOLESALE	Providing raw materials to wholesale suppliers is a widely used strategy in the refining or milling industry. For example, a wheat miller may sell its products to a wheat wholesaler.

WHAT IS A PRODUCT ROLLOUT?

When a company launches a new product into the market, it is known as a product rollout. The purpose of a rollout is to seamlessly integrate the product with the market and tap into the existing market share. A successful product launch is usually accompanied by an effective marketing campaign to attract potential consumers.

The following discussion will explore how to plan for a successful product launch.

PLANNING A SUCCESSFUL PRODUCT LAUNCH

Suppose you are a producer, manufacturer, or company launching a new product. In that case, you must stay on top of the launching plan to ensure the product is launched into the market effectively and seamlessly. Like your marketing strategy, creating a product launch plan is essential to ensure maximum success.

Let us explore the elements of a product launch or rollout plan.

PRE-LAUNCH

YOUR PRODUCT SHOULD WORK SEAMLESSLY

To ensure a successful product launch, the star of the show must perform flawlessly in every department. Therefore, verifying that the product you plan to market meets all quality assurance standards and serves its intended purpose is crucial before launching a product. By doing so, you can guarantee a successful product rollout.

DOUBLECHECK YOUR PRICING STRUCTURE

As you approach your product launch, you must evaluate your price point. Assess whether your product's value exceeds the cost to the consumer or if it is priced too high. Always remember that you should be able to defend your price point. Doing so establishes trust with your customers and shows that you offer them a fair deal.

UNDERSTAND YOUR CONSUMERS

To successfully launch your product, it is crucial to have a solid understanding of how the market will respond to it once it is released. This involves asking yourself important questions such as: What do your consumers like and dislike? Have there been similar products in the market before? If so, what sets your product apart from the competition? By clearly understanding your unique selling point, you will be better equipped to ensure that your product fits the market and resonates with your target audience. So do not hesitate to research and ask yourself the tough questions - it will ultimately help you achieve greater success in the market.

CREATE A POSITIONING STATEMENT

A well-crafted positioning statement is a powerful tool that enables a company to convey its unique selling points to its customers. It provides an irresistible explanation of what the company's product does and how it adds value. It is very similar to crafting a shark tank pitch, where you have to talk about your product with unwavering confidence for a minimum of 10 seconds, or even longer, to make a lasting impression.

PREPARE YOUR COMPANY

The core team responsible for launching your product must be fully engaged and informed about all the happenings. To ensure everyone is on the same page, providing them with a comprehensive list of questions and information about the product is advisable. This will enable them to communicate the new product's details effectively to others. Additionally, take advantage of the time you have to prepare your core team by discussing your positioning statement. This will allow you to make necessary improvements before presenting the statement to the consumers. By doing so, your message will be received with clarity and precision.

BETA TESTING

It is vital to consider the user's perspective when it comes to the effectiveness and usefulness of your product. One way to gauge that is by hiring beta testers to try your product in beta mode. While beta testing is commonly used in software development, tangible products can be tested using prototypes before the official launch. Doing so lets you gain valuable insights and feedback to improve your product before it hits the market.

After the beta testing phase, you must reach out to your testers and listen to their honest feedback. Their reviews will shape the perception of your product in the market. Do not miss this opportunity to fine-tune your offering and strengthen your market positioning. Show confidence in your product and ensure the feedback is used to improve it further.

SALES TEAM TRAINING

Training your sales team thoroughly as part of your product launch planning is imperative. Your entire organization must be aligned with the message you want to convey. Your sales team will be at the forefront of the launch, making it critical for them to be knowledgeable about the product and how to sell it. They should be well-informed about the product's features and capable of addressing consumers' queries. Additionally, they should be adept at using and troubleshooting the product seamlessly in case of any issues. With a well-prepared sales team, you can launch your product with the assurance that your team is fully equipped to deliver the best results.

LAUNCH

FACTORS TO CONSIDER BEFORE FINAL PRODUCT ROLLOUT:

Entrepreneurs, manufacturers, and producers face numerous challenges regarding product rollouts. However, a successful rollout is achievable with the right strategy and planning.

Even tech giants like Apple face product rollout hiccups at times. Take the example of the iPhone 6 Plus, which initially enjoyed a smooth rollout but later faced complaints about its vulnerability to bend and disabled cell service. This goes on to show that product rollout issues can occur to even the biggest companies in the world.

Therefore, it is crucial to have a solid strategy in place when planning a product rollout. You need to focus on three key components - distribution, timing, and promotion - and ensure that each is planned perfectly.

Disorganized timelines can hurt your company's credibility, and distribution issues can lead to wasted promotional efforts and poor sales numbers. To avoid this, educate the audience about your product and effectively deliver your company's message to build hype.

In addition, you need to have sufficient staff during the initial rollout phase, and your marketing campaign must be exciting. Your key vendors, distribution team, and providers should be aligned and prepared to scale up operations if needed.

Considering all these factors and ticking off the checklist below, you can determine if your product is ready for a successful rollout.

☑ MARKET RESEARCH

To succeed as a producer, you must deeply understand the market, particularly the one you aim to capture. Thorough market research is crucial to ensure your product meets customers' needs. Intuition is not enough; you must employ proper assessment tools to project revenues and gain insights into consumer behavior. Price modeling and customer segmentation are also vital components of effective market research. By conducting a comprehensive analysis, you can enter the market knowing that your product meets the demands of your target audience.

☑ MARKET TESTING

Successful product launches and effective market testing are two sides of the same coin, providing invaluable insights into the needs and preferences of your customers. By conducting thorough market testing, you can understand how your products will be used and what customers will pay for them. Furthermore, it enables you to identify gaps in your product's features and develop solutions to address any issues that may arise during use. With this knowledge at your fingertips, you can launch products that meet your customers' needs and maximize your chances of success.

☑ CHOOSE THE RIGHT OUTLET

Selecting the right media channel that best suits your brand and target audience is crucial when launching your product. With so many channels available, it is essential to identify the ones that will provide the maximum exposure and create a buzz around your product. Once you have zeroed in on the ideal media channel, ensure you have all your creative media ready - from social media posts to banners and posters - to make an impactful launch.

☑ REALISTIC TIMELINE

Efficiently scheduling your product rollout is of utmost importance. It is critical to ensure that the promotion and production of your product are in perfect alignment. Any misalignment can harm the rollout timeline. Therefore, creating a realistic rollout timeline aligned with market conditions and consumer demands is vital. You should consider critical factors such as testing, quality assurance, lead time for development, commercialization, and distribution to ensure a successful rollout. With a well-planned rollout, you can launch your product without worrying about your budget or reputation.

☑ INTERACTION WITH CUSTOMERS AND MEDIA

Now is the time to take charge and organize events such as press releases, exhibitions, and pop-ups. This is your opportunity to connect with your customers and influencers and give your brand a unique personality. By interacting directly with your target audience, you can gain invaluable feedback and give your product launch the boost it needs to skyrocket sales. So do not wait any longer; take the reins and make your mark in the market.

☑ CONTINGENCY PLANNING

Product rollouts are a vital part of any business, and while there may be some challenges along the way, it is essential to approach them with confidence. With proper planning, you can minimize the risk of any issues that may arise and have a contingency plan in place to address any unexpected problems quickly. Whether it is a shortage of supplies or a higher-than-anticipated demand, be prepared to handle any situation that comes your way. Remember, a seamless product rollout will help build your company's reputation and leave a lasting impression on consumers. So, do not hesitate to take the time to prepare and ensure you are ready to launch seamlessly. With hard work and dedication, you can capture your audience's excitement and showcase the product you have worked hard to develop.

POST-LAUNCH

No matter how much time and effort you put into crafting a product launch plan and executing it successfully, it is crucial to remember that the launch is just the beginning. To sustain the momentum, there are strategies you can implement post-launch. Additionally, the knowledge and experience you gain from this launch will be invaluable when launching your next product.

AVOID LOSING MOMENTUM

Once you successfully launch your product, it is crucial to maintain the momentum you have gained. Your sales team should be motivated to have frequent discussions and meetings to create and release fresh, shareable content that appeals to your target market. Doing this lets you keep building on the momentum you have already achieved, even after the launch.

Moreover, addressing all the feedback collected during the launch phase is essential and highlighting it in front of the customers. This will help establish trust in your brand and demonstrate that you value their feedback. Doing so can encourage customer loyalty and boost their purchasing behavior.

REVISIT AND EVALUATE YOUR MARKETING PLAN

Once the launch is over, evaluating your marketing plan and its results is always wise. You must assess whether the marketing plan gave you what you were looking for or fell short in any particular area. To measure your success, you should compare your real numbers against the reports and potential numbers you or your team highlighted earlier. This will tell you whether your marketing tactics and tools were successful, and if they were not, you can change them to improve your next launch.

Remember, no matter how well you execute your product launch, there is always room for improvement, and you should be able to identify and improve upon those areas. So, evaluate your entire process with a confident mindset to learn from your mistakes and gain motivation from your successes. Ask yourself what areas need to be improved, what you did well, what you should have avoided in this launch, and most importantly, what you learned about future launches. With a detailed evaluation, you can ensure that your future launches will be even more successful than your previous ones.

FOCUS ON CUSTOMER RETENTION

A successful launch requires a great product, the right people, and a plan to maintain momentum. You must invest your effort, time, and resources in customer retention strategies and practical steps to keep your product launch successful. One effective way to accomplish this is by creating an easy-to-understand FAQ section or user guide to help customers with any questions or issues.

Your aftersales support should be exceptional, even if the customer is dissatisfied with the product. Your team must always be on standby and have the necessary knowledge to troubleshoot any issues. Additionally, your feedback channels should always remain open and available for customers to provide you with valuable insights about the product. This will help you gain their trust and address any issues for future product launches.

It is essential to understand that a successful product launch requires a combination of elements such as the right people, execution, and, most importantly, the right product. However, preparing for mistakes and missed deadlines is crucial because we are all human. Despite the challenges, you must remain prepared for anything that comes your way.

CHAPTER 10

DEMONSTRATING SUCCESS

ENSURING PRODUCT SUCCESS BY COLLECTING FEEDBACK AND MAKING IM-PROVEMENTS (IF NEED BE).

In the previous chapter, we emphasized the critical role of post-launch activities in ensuring a business's product launch success. One of the most crucial aspects of customer retention is recognizing the significance of customer feedback. Let us delve deeper into how customer feedback can be leveraged to drive improvements and sustain your product's success.

IMPORTANCE OF CUSTOMER FEEDBACK

Your product has been successfully launched, and your customer satisfaction strategies are in place. You have worked hard to ensure your customers are happy, and your aftersales and support teams are doing everything possible to satisfy them. However, you must focus on customer feedback to know if your customer service is working.

Obtaining customer feedback is crucial for any business, as it helps you understand your customers' expectations and requirements. It allows you to identify areas of improvement and build a loyal customer base. By communicating with your customers and evaluating their responses, you can create a product that meets their needs and surpasses their expectations. So, do not hesitate to seek customer feedback and use it to your advantage.

It is the key to your company's success.

WHY DO YOU NEED CUSTOMER FEEDBACK?

Customer feedback is an integral part of any successful business. It is not just an optional task that can be sidelined because it can make or break your company's reputation. By listening to your customers, you can gain valuable insights that can help you improve your product development, operations, marketing strategies, and more. Without feedback, you may not be able to build the right customer base, which can hurt your sales and lead to an inability to keep up with the changing needs of your customers.

It is essential to understand that listening to your customers and acting upon their feedback is the best way to enhance your brand's image. It builds trust between you and the customer, making them feel heard and valued. Furthermore, customers expect a brand to deliver precisely what is being advertised. Any discrepancy between the product description and the actual product can lead to customer frustration and a sense of betrayal. Therefore, aligning your product offerings with your brand's message is imperative.

Focusing on multiple business projects without reviewing customer feedback can be detrimental to your company's image. If you ignore what your customers say about your product or service, you cannot keep up with the dynamic consumer market. By obtaining honest customer feedback (qualitative and quantitative), you can better understand the product marketplace and make informed decisions for the future.

REASONS FOR COLLECTING CUSTOMER FEEDBACK

1. To understand your customers
2. To improve your product
3. To engage with customers
4. To gather honest reviews and testimonials
5. To evaluate and enhance strategies

WHAT IS CUSTOMER FEEDBACK?

Customer feedback is an essential element that can make or break a business. It provides valuable insights into a client's satisfaction or dissatisfaction with products, services, employees, company policies, and the overall shopping experience. By taking immediate action on feedback, businesses can improve their operations and provide customers with the utmost satisfaction, resulting in a seamless customer experience.

To succeed in today's competitive market, it is crucial to research and understand customers' perceptions of the brand and the product. Listening to their voices and acting upon their feedback is the best way to improve their experience and build a strong customer base. This approach will help establish customer loyalty and drive purchasing behavior toward your company, ultimately moving your business forward.

BEST WAYS TO COLLECT CUSTOMER FEEDBACK

Collecting customer feedback does not necessarily have to be limited to one-on-one conversations. Call centers are a crucial component of customer interactions as they have the potential to gather vital customer feedback. The information provided by call centers presents a significant opportunity for business-es to improve themselves. With their wide clientele range, call centers offer valuable insights into enhancing every aspect of your business.

If your business aims to provide customers with products they need, acting upon consumer feedback is the best way to go. Consider customer feedback a powerful tool influencing your decision-making and innovations to create better products and services. This tool is essential for your business to rank high on the customer satisfaction meter. General customer feedback also measures the satisfaction level among your brand's current customers, which can help you extrapolate your position in the market. By understanding how your customers view your product or support your brand, you can easily influence their decisions and increase your overall revenue.

Here's what you can do:

- Gathering crucial information like your customers' email addresses and phone numbers should be a top priority when selling your product. This enables you to create a compre-hensive database and mailing list, which can be utilized for future marketing efforts.
- Regularly calling your customers and asking them how the product works for them is a great habit to develop. Not only does it show your confidence in the product, but it also al-lows you to make improvements and adjustments based on their feedback.
- Your website must have a live chat support system that empowers customers to resolve their queries quickly and

efficiently, even if they cannot get through a phone call or do not prefer verbal communication.

- To ensure you provide your customers with the best possible support, you must save and monitor all live chat support sessions. Doing so will enable you to gain valuable insights into customers' most common issues with your product. Armed with this information, you can proactively address these issues and ensure your customers are always satisfied with your service.

- By investing in social learning and closely monitoring your customers' social media activity, you can gain valuable insights into the reviews they give your product on their platforms. This will enable you to confidently assess the impact of your product and make informed decisions about how to improve it to serve your customers better.

- Take control of your online presence with Google alerts. By setting up alerts for your brand or product name, you can stay on top of any content published about you. Be in the know about your business's online progress and confidently monitor your success.

- Creating an online community or forum for customers to actively post questions, polls, and queries related to the product or product line would be a highly strategic move.

- If you want to be sure of the effectiveness of your customer service, using customer service performance analytic tools is a must. With these analytical tools, you can easily monitor your customer service system and access all the necessary information to make it flawless and highly effective.

- Utilizing your email listing can be an effective way to send email services regarding your products. This approach can involve inquiring your customers about the future improvements they would like to see and what aspect of the product intrigues them the most. Doing so lets you gather valuable insights and feedback to improve your product and meet your customers' needs.

- Gathering feedback forms is absolutely necessary as it enables customers to express their honest opinions without hesitation. Classifying these forms into distinct categories, such as complaints, suggestions, appreciations, and so on, is crucial for better analysis. Doing this lets you use the feedback received to enhance your business.

- By assessing your competitor's customer feedback strategies, you can gain valuable insights to evaluate and improve your strategy. Analyzing what your competitors are doing that you are not can help you identify potential gaps and opportunities to strengthen your feedback methods.

- Encouraging customers to provide product feedback can be effectively done by offering them incentives. Whether it is a discount or a gift, providing an incentive can boost the chances of customers submitting a feedback form, which can help you gather more insights and improve your products or services.

- Dealing with negative feedback like a professional is a must-have skill. Expecting 100% positive feedback from everyone is unrealistic, but handling negative feedback positively and maintaining a fair brand image is essential. So, respond positively and show your customers you are committed to providing the best service possible.

If you have gathered all the necessary information, make improvements wherever required. Regardless of your business's level of success, there is always room for progress and development.

Let us explore some practical ways to sustain your business's triumph and enhance it in areas that require attention.

BUSINESS IMPROVEMENT STRATEGIES

Consistently improving your business is crucial to staying ahead of the competition and achieving long-term success. Regularly monitoring your cash flow and leveraging social media for effective marketing can strengthen your brand and establish a reputation as a leader in your industry. Identifying your strengths will enable you to focus your efforts and resources on areas that yield maximum results and drive growth. To keep your business on the right track, maintain a checklist of essential tasks that promote ongoing evaluation and improvement. Follow these guidelines to ensure that your business continues to thrive:

KEEP FINANCIAL TABS

Very few businesses in the market accurately know their financial numbers going in and out weekly or monthly. You should always keep a score of all financial processes going on in your business so that you have an accurate idea of where you stand. You should divert the necessary effort and time towards keeping an updated cash flow. However, if you do not possess financial skills, you can always hire an accountant to manage your books and accounts.

SET BUSINESS GOALS

Setting clear business goals and objectives is crucial to driving your business towards greater success. Establishing these goals allows you to create a solid plan to propel your business forward continuously. This approach enables you to focus on your vision for the future and turn it into reality. It is important to constantly strive for more orders, traffic, sales, and increased customer loyalty. With a steady and persistent effort, you can achieve all these goals and take your business to new heights of success.

KEEP EVALUATING YOUR MARKETING

Effective marketing is key to the success of any business, but it is too easy to waste money on tactics that do not deliver results. That is why focusing on high-impact strategies that will not drain your budget is crucial. Do not settle for mediocre marketing efforts - aim for greatness by testing two to three new tactics and implementing the ones that perform best.

Social media marketing is one of the most cost-effective and low-risk options when promoting your business. Be sure to leverage the power of platforms like Instagram, Facebook, LinkedIn, and X (Twitter) to build your brand and attract new customers.

But do not make the mistake of thinking that marketing is a one-and-done activity. It is an ongoing process that requires consistent effort and innovation. Keep your campaigns fresh and engaging, and always look for new opportunities to connect with your audience.

And remember - the work does not stop once you have launched your marketing campaigns. Regularly evaluate your strategies and solicit customer feedback to ensure you deliver top-quality experiences that meet their needs and exceed their expectations. With the right mindset and approach, you can build a marketing strategy that drives growth and success for your business.

MONITOR MARKET TRENDS

In today's fast-changing business landscape, watching the market trends and changes happening locally and globally is imperative. Operating in isolation is no longer an option for businesses as the market is dynamic and ever-evolving. By monitoring every factor that impacts the market and the local community, you and your team can stay ahead of the curve and anticipate potential challenges. Even if a particular factor is not affecting your business presently, evaluating its probable future impact is crucial. This proactive approach will help your business stay relevant and adapt to changing consumer preferences. So, keep an open mind and consider all possibilities, as it can make all the difference in the competitive business world.

FOCUS ON YOUR SALES TEAM

Mastering the sales function of a business can pave the way for unprecedented profits, which can be achieved with a suitable set of skills. Keep polishing your selling skills, regardless of the size of your sales team. Even if you are a one-person army, prioritize sales improvement as a major goal. Once you have laid out a clear vision and purpose for your business, ensure that the sales function has enough training and knowledge to attract more clients. Just like there is always room for improvement in a business, there is always room for employee training.

PROMOTE TRANSPARENCY

To ensure the success of your business, you must maintain a high level of ethics and transparency in all your operations. Documenting all communication, testing, and other business activities is essential to avoid misunderstandings and ethical dilemmas. Adopting these practices allows you to run your business seamlessly, overcome obstacles, and efficiently achieve your goals.

STAFF MOTIVATION

A business with motivated staff will perform better and achieve greater success. Therefore, attracting and retaining talented and motivated employees should be a top priority for any business that aims to reach higher performance levels. It is essential to provide your employees a platform to express their opinions and ideas, regardless of their experience level or seniority. By actively listening to their input, you can make them feel valued and appreciated, ultimately leading to better business outcomes. Who knows what brilliant ideas may come from the employees who work with you? So, create an environment that encourages them to speak up, and you may be surprised by its positive impact on your business.

ASSESS YOUR WEAKNESSES

To be a successful business owner and ensure the smooth operation of your business, you must identify and address your weaknesses. For instance, if accounting is not your strongest suit and your expertise lies in sales, it is wise to enlist the services of an external expert to handle your books while you focus on what you do best - driving sales. Recognizing and embracing your limitations does not make you any less capable. In fact, it shows that you are pragmatic in your approach to business. Remember, every business owner has weaknesses; the key is identifying them and proactively finding effective solutions.

CLOSING THOUGHTS AND TAKEAWAYS

Mastering the FMCG product business can be challenging due to its highly competitive and complex nature. With several dynamic stepping stones between you and your consumer, the entire scope of events may initially seem overwhelming. However, managing every aspect of the process is essential to take a product from concept to commercialization. The key is to remain focused and determined and strive for excellence at every stage of the journey.

It is perfectly fine to start slow and take your time to think through things. However, in the early stages, you should be confident in your investments and capital expenditure decisions. Consider it carefully, but do not be afraid to take bold steps toward success.

As you leap from one pillar to another, remember that each new stage in business planning presents its intricacies, expectations, rules, and practices. However, these aspects are collectively more crucial than the quality of the product itself, particularly when introducing new products. So, focus on mastering these fundamentals to succeed in your business ventures.

Armed with the knowledge of Concept to Commercialization of FMCG Products, you will be fully equipped with the necessary skills and expertise most new entrepreneurs lack. This will prepare you to become a confident product entrepreneur who can fearlessly penetrate the highly competitive product business world.

Establishing a product in the market is not only lucrative, but it also has the potential to become a consistent source of long-term revenue. Adopting the right methods and approaches can generate a substantial income that can increase exponentially over time. For instance, if you could generate $1 million in revenue during your first year, you could potentially sell your business for a minimum of $3 to $6 million. It is all about having the right mindset and strategies to make your business grow and succeed.

With the concepts outlined in this book, you have the power to make a significant impact in the market. Your ultimate business goal should be centered around empowering others and gaining recognition for your brand. This way, you can establish your FMCG product company as a marketing, design, and branding leader while fostering positive consumer relationships. With this mindset, success is not only achievable but inevitable.

If you have followed all the necessary steps, congratulations! You are ready to take your FMCG product concept to commercialization, which is no small feat. It is time to turn your dream into a reality and ensure your business runs like a well-oiled machine with all its wheels turning. Do not forget to refine the rough edges and rejuvenate each component to set your sights on a profitable and prosperous future. With your hard work and dedication, you have everything it takes to make it happen!

Skipping these crucial steps can put the foundation of your business at risk. Revisiting critical business details such as incentives, pricing, partner deals, and marketing is imperative to ensure everything runs smoothly without hiccups. By doing so, you can ensure the success of your business and avoid potential pitfalls down the road.

Your product must embody a challenge and hold immense potential for success. You can achieve wealth and fame by adhering to the vital lessons outlined in this book. While we have covered tangible factors that can be implemented for your employees or distributors, ultimately, the success and experience of your business are in your hands. So, with unwavering confidence, put your heart and soul into the game and enjoy the ride to the top!

REFERENCES

Alibaba. (2019). Find Quality Manufacturers, Suppliers, Exporters, Importers, Buyers, Wholesalers, Products, and Trade Leads from Our Award-Winning International Trade Site. https://www.alibaba.com/

H. (2020). *Customer Feedback Software | HubSpot.* Hubspot. https://www.hubspot.com/products/service/customer-feedback?_ga=2.123102153.354090664.1562599537-933118289.1529345498&hubs_post=blog.hubspot.com%2Fservice%2Fconcept-testing&hubs_post-cta=feedback%20collection%20tools

IndiaMART. (2021). *IndiaMART.* Indian Manufacturers Suppliers Exporters Directory, India Exporter Manufacturer. https://www.indiamart.com/

Kompass International. (2016). Global B2B Portal to Find & Contact Products or Services Suppliers. https://www.kompass.com/selectcountry/

Maker's Row. (2019). Manufacturing Software, Sourcing, Production Education. https://makersrow.com/

MFG. (2021, March 15). *MFG.* The World's Largest Custom Manufacturing Marketplace. https://www.mfg.com/

NAM. (2021). Workforce Solutions. https://www.nam.org/workforce-solutions/directory/

Nielsen | Audience is Everything. (2021). Neilson. https://www.nielsen.com/pk/en/

Pincombe, J. (2021, June 17). *Product Development Services - R&D - Innovation | Innovolo*. Innovolo Ltd. https://innovolo.co.uk/

Shopify. (2020). Find Products to Sell Online with Oberlo. https://www.shopify.com/oberlo

Sourcify. (2020, April 17). Product Sourcing Simplified. https://www.sourcify.com/

Techopedia. (2017, June 9). *Prototype*. Techopedia.Com. https://www.techopedia.com/definition/678/prototype

Thomasnet. (2020). Product Sourcing and Supplier Discovery Platform - Find North American Manufacturers, Suppliers and Industrial Companies. https://www.thomasnet.com/

Upwork Global Inc. (2021). *Upwork*. The World's Work Marketplace for Freelancing. https://www.upwork.com/

ABOUT THE AUTHOR

Manal Haddad's journey is a testament to the power of hard work and continuous learning. He is an accomplished business professional with extensive experience in sales, marketing, business development, and consulting. He has managed multinational organizations and international brands and has led cross-cultural teams to success. Today, Manal uses his knowledge and expertise to help business owners develop high-growth strategies and reach their goals. As a passionate mentor, he is committed to inspiring the next generation of leaders and empowering them with the knowledge and skills they need to impact the world positively. He believes in sharing knowledge to shape a better future. His writings reflect his enthusiasm and dedication to helping individuals pursue their entrepreneurial dreams. He is the author of several books on marketing, sales, distribution, process implementation, and leadership.

In his personal life, Manal is a devoted husband and father. He relishes listening to the freedom of expression in Jazz and feeling the thrill of cruising on his motorcycle on the open road in his free time. Visit him at

www.manalhaddad.com.

www.ingramcontent.com/pod-product-compliance
Lightning Source LLC
Chambersburg PA
CBHW060629290526
45793CB00001B/204